I0429645

COUPLES THERAPHY WORKBOOKS

The Never Seen Before Questions and Conversation Starters to Build Emotional Intimacy and Reconnect with Your Partner

© Written by: Katerina Griffith

©Copyright 2022 Katerina Griffith All rights reserved

The content within this book may not be reproduced, duplicated, or transmitted without direct written permission from the author or the publisher.

Under no circumstances will any blame or legal responsibility be held against the publisher, or author, for any damages, reparation, or monetary loss due to the information contained within this book, either directly or indirectly.

Legal Notice

This book is copyright protected. This book is only for personal use. You cannot amend, distribute, sell, use, quote, or paraphrase any part, or the content within this book, without the consent of the author-publisher.

Disclaimer Notice

Please note that the information contained within this document is for educational and entertainment purposes only. All effort has been executed to present accurate, up-to-date, and reliable, complete information. No warranties of any kind are declared or implied. Readers acknowledge that the author is not engaging in the rendering of legal, financial, medical, or professional advice.

TABLE OF CONTENTS

PREFACE

Every human has the need for acceptance. There is a burning desire to be seen as satisfactory both by one's self and by other. First comes self-acceptance. This is the approval, validation, appreciation and support of the self as it is. It is the satisfaction and self-appreciation that comes after examining one's self. When a person is satisfied and accepting of his/herself, there arises a need to be accepted by others as a part of a whole. Over time, relationships begin to form and there comes along with it a conscious effort to make it fruitful, worthwhile, special. We as humans often needs support from one another; emotionally, physically, financial, psychological support and its highly logical to want it with someone or people whom we admire and value so much. Building intimacy and connections of any kind often takes time, guidance, dedication, resilience. Conversations needs to be had, questions need to be asked, opinions heard, all for adequate and complete understanding of each other. We are all different, came from different backgrounds, had different roots and level of exposure, so going into any relationship is more or less like walking to a new school, blank sheets of paper, ready to take notes, learn from each other and eventually graduate to become a successful student. However, education and learning doesn't stop at any point. We learn new things everyday so our banner of enthusiasm has to always fly, hence a guide to building emotional intimacy and relationships.

INTRODUCTION

Intimacy

There is a general desire to belong and to love in every human which is usually satisfied in an intimate relationship. Humans are social animals that thrive when in contact with each other, thus the need for intimate relationships. The desire for intimacy has been programmed into the genetic engineering of the human body, it is more often than not, a prerequisite for happiness; true happiness which comes not from possession or pleasure but from the satisfaction of a deep rooted urge for intimacy. The brain releases Endorphins which are neurotransmitters that puts one in a similar euphoric state as recreational drugs, these natural chemicals are released into the blood stream when one experiences feelings of elation and joy which are emotions that are often rewards of an affective intimate relationship. These chemical responses are easily physically and emotionally addictive which is why people often develop the need to create and maintain an intimate relationship with each other or in small groups. In its purest form, intimacy is a complete unrestrained sharing of self. It is the process of mutual self revelation that inspires a level of trust and openness deeper than normal interpersonal relationships. It illuminates points of strengths, points of weaknesses, true feelings about events and experiences, failings, hopes, dreams, fears, flaws, abilities, potentials, phobias, e. t. c.

The need for intimacy among people results from an desire to be part of a whole. Intimacy in a relationship brings a sense of closeness and emotional connection through which partners are able to share through feelings, thoughts and experiences. Intimacy grows in the absence of emotional independence, it requires the merging of one's self with another, lowering of barriers and reservations to allow partners be their truest self in a safe space devoid of criticism and personal opinions to create a deeper level of understanding and intimacy between them. Understanding intimacy entails more of feelings about experiences than the experiences itself; it is more of an emotional phenomenon than a physical one. It is relatively easy to confide in your partner about an experience, but a certain level of intimacy has to be reached to effectively communicate to your partner how those experiences made you feel. Intimacy is crucial to basic human functioning. Research has shown that human beings are more productive, innovative, and creative when they are in a "safe space ". This is one of the rewards of intimacy, it gives the opportunity for one to express and share ideas with each other or among themselves in the case of a group.

Apart from the satisfaction and freedom to express ones true desire or fear that intimacy provides, it also creates a safe space for rehabilitation of individuals. The absence of aggression and critical judgment in an intimate gathering helps recovering addicts to overcome addictions. Addicts anonymous (AA) gatherings provide a safe empathic environment for recovering addicts, it helps to create a safe space where intimate relationships can be formed between a small group of people experiencing the same reality. The idea of empathy and understanding without criticism creates a sense of closeness, an feeling of being a part of something bigger than one's self and this encourages the formation of intimate relationships among them which helps in rehabilitation.

The drive for intimate contact gradually grows and etch itself in deeper in various areas of one's life. When desired intimacy is achieved, the likelihood for happiness and contentment drastically increases. Then intimacy expands and evolve over time. It is fueled by a slow release of trust, openness, understanding and the desire to feel closer to another being on a deeper level. One doesn't just form an intimate relationship with one's partner, intimacy comes in different forms, depending on the kind and effectiveness of communication and shared ideas existing between individuals.

Emotional intimacy is then created between partners in a sexual relationship. Emotional intimacy depends mainly on trust, the degree of affection between partners and the closeness they share which allows them to express feelings effectively both in verbal and non verbal communication. Partners with strong a strong emotional intimacy can be easily identified because of their interactions with each other. There is usually a sync of communication between them, understanding without explanation, constant show of affection like touching as often as possible, holding hands, and a sense of togetherness between them. Emotional intimacy usually involves the satisfaction and confidence of one's inner thoughts and fears being known and accepted without prejudice. It is essential for intimacy to be maintained in a sexual relationship for its success. Research carried out in the US shows that 10% of married couples divorce within 5 years and 20% of married couples divorce within 10 years. One rampant reason for the high rate of divorce is the lack of emotional intimacy between partners. During the early romantic illusion stage of a marriage or an emotional relationship, there usually is a false sense of perfect fit, unconditional love, support, encouragement and stability. This is mostly because the brain pleasure zones kick in when love is new, everything seems lighter and brighter because of the natural chemicals that flows when one experiences feelings of elation and joy. Over time, these sense become duller and those little moments that used to bring excitement becomes tedious and this causes frustration and uneasiness between partners. You begin to feel like your partner has changed, activities that used to excite you becomes a bore, not because you do not enjoy them anymore but because there are many underlying issues that needs to be addressed. Couples that have built emotional intimacy over time will find it easier to navigate through these issues and successfully resolve them which helps to strengthen their relationship over time. Couples with emotional intimacy are also more at ease with each other because of their shared vulnerability. They are able to confidently discuss both positive and negative thoughts and feelings to each other because of the level of transparency and trust between them. However, Couples that do not have emotional intimacy between them will find it hard to allow themselves be vulnerable with each other and share their fears and feelings because there is an absence of a safe space for them to share their feelings without criticism and condemnation, also a lack of trust, poor communication and hidden emotions. When these underlying issues are not properly addressed, resentment begin to grow in place of affection, loving sentiments give way to constant complaining, and both partners begin to feel like they have made a mistake, rather than working harmoniously to create a conducive environment to solve the problem and for intimacy to grow between them, one or both partners move to terminate the relationship.

CREATING AND MAINTAINING EMOTIONAL INTIMACY

Creating and maintaining intimacy is crucial for the maintenance and growth of one's relationship. It requires genuine interest, transparency, vulnerability and reciprocity. The degree of intimacy in a relationship is determined by the ability to listen to and understand one's partner. Emotional intimacy requires deep level of connection and intimacy which is held together by open effective communication. Emotional intimacy involves a level of vulnerability and confidence which is absolutely necessary and needed for the formation of trust which is necessary for partners in a new relationship to have in order to form genuine emotional intimacy between them. Couples in an intimate relationship must develop genuine interest to create intimacy and be willing to lower their emotional barriers and be vulnerable with each other. This requires a certain level of commitment and trust. When one partner does not match the level of trust needed to maintain an intimate relationship, the relationship scale is tipped, and the individual on the lower end becomes defensive and assuming. In this state, true intimacy between such partners cannot be reached. There is also a need for a certain level of transparency, common interest and shared goal between them. Emotional intimacy is a prerequisite to building a long lasting relationship, and such intimacies are built through open effective communications between partners. The need for effective communication on building emotional intimacy cannot be over emphasized. It is only when partners have an open line of communication between them that they are able to build and maintain emotional intimacy. Maintain emotional intimacy takes hard work and dedication with a effective open line of communication between partners.

THE EMOTIONAL INTIMACY SCALE

According to the Sinclair development and validation of Emotional Intimacy scale, the Emotional intimacy scale examines the level of emotional intimacy present between partners in an intimate relationship. The Emotional Intimacy Scale (EIS) seeks to answer five (5) questions to determine the level of intimacy between partners.

1. Does my partner completely accepts me as I am?

2. Can I confidently discuss my deepest thoughts and fears with my partner?

3. Does my partner genuinely care for me?

4. Is my partner willing to help me overcome my personal problems and fears in any way?

5. Are my deepest thoughts and feelings completely understood and accepted by my partner?

The above questions when answered, illuminates on the presence or absence of emotional intimacy between partners. The Emotional intimacy scale also shows that an intimate relationship gives a sense of purpose and togetherness which helps to improve the physiological and psychological well-being of an individual.

EMPATHY AND EMPATHIC BOND

An important part of building and maintaining an emotional intimate relationship is having feelings of empathy towards each other. Couples need to build an Empathic Bond with each other in other to create and maintain an intimate relationship. The Empathic bond between partners helps them to hear and understand each other's feelings without criticism or Empathic feelings also helps to maintain a steady intimate relationship and keep the emotional intimacy scale balanced. Being empathic towards ones partner involves being aware of the emotional and physiological state your partner is in and relating to it without judgment. Having empathy allows you to "put yourself in the other shoe" to fully understand the message your partner is communicating. Partners in an intimate relationship, when sharing deep thoughts and ideas, need to develop a sense of empathy with each other. This allows them to fully understand both the said and unsaid messages one's partner is passing across; it makes them more self aware and in accord with the feelings of their significant other. Being empathic doesn't mean offering suggestions to fix personal problems of one's partner, it means understanding that your partner is going through a rough patch and offering a listening ear and safe haven to expressly share deep thoughts without interruption; it also involves putting aside ones views and values on issues bothering your partner and being completely in tune with their own feelings and thoughts. When partners are empathic towards one another, a deep feeling of understanding and unwavering support grows between them and the relationship becomes stronger. Offering advice and personal opinions on deep thoughts and feelings of one's partner, however thoughtful or helpful it may be, might cause your partner to feel like they have to defend themselves which may destroy the idea of a safe haven for them to share feelings and thoughts. These personal opinions, thoughts and advice might come across to them as condescending and patronizing. This may cause them to bottle up such thoughts in the future and lead to resentment, thus tipping the emotional intimacy scale.

Though a person might not fully understand what his / her significant other is going through, just listening and being completely in the moment with him / her comes across as a gesture of comfort and support. Partners in an intimate relationship need to feel supported by each other in other for them to grow together in harmony with one another. There is a desire for interdependence in relationships, partners want to attain a deeper level of connection with each other that builds feelings of unwavering faith, support and trust in each other. They need to trust that they can depend on their significant other in times of need and comfort. It is in this state of togetherness (whatever it is, we are in it together) that connections between partners grows deeper than stronger; their need for closeness and intimacy is being satisfied in such moments.

When partners have shared interests, they spend more time together or in the same space which can help in strengthening the level of intimacy between them. Having empathy for your partner's feelings and thoughts shows your significant other that you are committed to helping him / her, that you care and you are willing to do whatever it takes to help them feel better. It shows that you accept them wholly; this includes accepting all positive and negative thoughts, fears, feelings, their ideologies, their behavioral quirks and idiosyncrasies and helping them feel accepted.

RESENTMENT

Over time, couples may start to generate feeling of insecurities in certain areas of their life and feel the urge to confide in one's partner. The response of the partner being confided in can either help to strengthen or weaken the relationship. Responding with scathing remarks (example : you are being silly) might cause one's partner to be defensive and unwilling to share anymore. Such response goes in contrast to the need to the partner to feel accepted. Even when such feelings are not completely understood, it is important to accept them as what your partner is going through and offer physical and emotional support, not simply dismissing them as just another "quirk".

When partners in a relationship begin to feel like they are not being heard or acknowledged in the relationship, feelings of resentment quickly blooms between them and the couple begins to fight for the right to receive empathy. Both parties develops a sense of entitlement and bicker over whose experience deserve sympathy and whose do not. The couple begin to keep scores over fights, have unrealistic expectations of each other, becomes passive aggressive, vengeful, and judgmental. They begin to have different expectations of the relationship and aim at winning fights rather than settling differences. They withhold affection and consciously or unconsciously trying to hurt each other with hurtful words and snide comments. There is little or no physical contact and partners being to feel separate from each other. Communication between them is minimal or non existent and reserved for just the necessary. There is a lack of compromise in such relationships, absence of kindness and even small talk begins to feel confrontational instead of conversational. If not dealt with immediately, resentment tends to accumulate and it becomes harder to empathize with one's partner because of the feeling of self righteousness and justification that makes it difficult for them to care about each others experiences and feelings. Gradually, all feelings of intimacy and tenderness dissolves and it becomes impossible for a healthy relationship to survive. Resentment grows on continual unresolved disappointments

Feelings of resentments arising from unfulfilled needs for adjustment, lack of empathy among partners and unmet expectations of the relationship can cause partners to drift apart from each other, create an emotional distance between them, and break their chain of connection. When there is an emotional distance between partners, the ideology of give and take that makes relationships run smoothly becomes eroded; healthy relationships are based on reciprocity in partners, a give and take process, and when this is lost, the relationship becomes one-sided and resentment grows. Partners being to loose trust in their significant other's capability to provide the love and support they need in the relationship, then they too stop giving and this affects the commitment to the relationship. A lack of commitment in the relationship gives partners an excuse to spend less and less time with and around each other. They begin to develop separate interests which sometimes can be a good idea, but when there is no common interest between couples, they start to feel lonely in the relationship and estrangement occurs which could potentially lead to permanent separation.

Resentment inspires a sense of self protection and independence among couples. They develop preventive measures to protect themselves from being emotional hurt by their partner. The need to protect ones self in an emotional relationship, is in contrast to the idea of intimacy which inspires closeness between the couple. When one or both partners begin to feel the need for self protection, it creates an emotional and physical distance. The emotional distance between partners does not fulfill the basic need for closeness and intimacy, couples loose the sense of "belonging" in the relationship and begin to feel separate and alone.

RECONNECTING RELATIONSHIPS

The absence of emotional intimacy between couples creates a feeling of isolation. One or both partners begin to feel indifferent towards the feelings of the other, which will cause them to drift apart. In this state, couples have to either agree to try to reconnect their relationship or terminate it.

Couples willing to reconnect their relationship must let of of grudges and scores from previous fights and aim at complete reconciliation. Reconnecting relationships involves developing a feeling of empathy and reciprocity; relationships are stable when both partners practice a give and take ritual. Both parties depend on each other for affection and support, and when they realize they both need the same things out of the relationship, it becomes easier for them to navigate through their issues and successfully give what they are asking to receive. Couples who have drifted apart cannot be successful reconnected if one of both of them is not willing to forgive and move on. It is almost impossible to regenerate feelings of love and affection from a non cooperative partner still holding on to a grudge. Partners have to desire the reconnection and be ready to put effort into sustaining it. Reconnection in a relationship doesn't completely ensure the absence of disagreement on issues concerning the couple, the couple have to learn to compromise, meet each other half way, and arrive at a win-win solution to problems. Recreating feelings of intimacy between estranged partners requires having a heart to heart conversation with both parties. Previous causes of disagreement might arise again and though partners might not agree with each others points of view, it is important to make an effort to listen to what your partner is saying. Listening to one's partner can help attain a deeper level of understanding, which may lead to development of empathic feelings towards ones partner. The idea behind reconnecting relationships is not to point out who was right and who was wrong about issues, but to help partners willing to give their relationship a second chance rediscover the intimacies and joy of an emotional satisfying relationship.

Making an emotional relationship a lasting success requires genuine interest, a shared goal and willingness to work through issues from both partners. They have to be ready to recreate the love and attraction they once shared in order to keep the relationship alive.

One major reason for estrangement between partners is a deficiency in communication and a lack of communication skills. During reconnection, couples have to be open and honest about their feelings and thoughts towards each other. Effectively Communicating one's expectations from the relationship and the feelings they inspired can be a bit tricky because partners have to take care to share thoughts and fear without attaching blame. When partners in the process of reconnecting their relationship start nitpicking and assigning blame and criticism over previous disagreements, they tend to loose the feeling of empathy towards each other in a bid to defend themselves, and the need for them to understand each others needs, feelings and thoughts to effectively reconnect is lost.

Assigning blame in the guise of self expression produces a contrast effect to the idea of open effective communication and reconnection because it gives room for partners to slip back to their original behaviors and puts them on opposing sides rather than the same side with a shared goal. It creates an argumentative exchange between partners ("I did this because you did that ", "I didn't do that because you didn't do that", or "I said this because it felt bad when you said that"). This may cause old feelings of resentment to rise up again; when couples begin to feel like they have to constantly defend their actions rather than explaining them, the emotional distance between the couple continues to widen causing them to drift further apart. . Openly criticizing your partner might cause him/her to be defensive and standoffish. They might begin to feel attacked and respond with aggression, trying to point out the other partner's mistakes too which will lead to a full blown argument. It is important to express to express emotions without putting partners on opposing sides. The motive behind expressing feelings and thoughts during reconnection is not assign blames, see who is right or who is wrong and who wins the fight. The motive behind this is to allow both partners see each others point of view. During heated arguments, both parties might be too caught up in their own feelings of justification to allow them see their partner's perspective which doesn't necessarily have to be right or wrong, but can help them understand and empathize with each other.

When aiming at reconnection, it is important for both parties to focus on themselves rather than what the other party said or did; when couples focus on their own feelings, it takes them away from rehashing out previous disagreements and assigning blame. Instead, couples should focus on events and experiences that created the emotional distance between them and the feelings brought on by those experiences. By doing this, it gives a chance for both parties to fully express themselves and see from each others perspective which gives room for better understanding.

Reconnecting relationships entails having in depth conversation about situations and experiences that made one or both partners feel hurt or disappointed with the aim of rebuilding lost feelings of affection, support and intimacy. During reconnection, partners have to fully express how certain experiences made them feel without dismissing even the most minute feeling of hurt as an overreaction. The aim of this is to allow the other partner fully understand the extent to which previous experiences affected their significant other causing them to drift apart, thereby eliminating the risks of repetition of such events.

Unmet expectations could also result in emotional distance between couples. When couples begin to feel restless and unsatisfied with their relationship, it creates a bridge between them. Dissatisfaction in a relationship does not necessarily mean your partner is incapable for meeting your needs. Sometimes, partners do not even know what the their significant other expects from the relationship and they just do what they think will please the other person without knowing exactly what they want. Over time, dissatisfaction builds up into restlessness and the dissatisfied partner begin to feel disconnected from the relationship and his/ her partner. In order to reconnect with each other, couples have to clearly state their wants and expectations from the relationship and from each other. They have to be clear on both their personal and joint expectations; when couples understand what they both want from each other, common issues that usually results in disagreements becomes inconsequential. This process allows both partners to be more attuned with themselves and introduce a sense of closeness between them. Clearly stating one's expectations in a relationship, If done wrongly could do more harm than good in reconnecting partners. The method of approach when stating one's expectations is very important because it dictates your partner's response to those unmet expectations. It is highly unlikely that couples will respond positively to each other expectations if it is stated in an irritable and complaining manner. Confiding in one's partner about one's expectations in a relationship should not be done in a whiny manner, demanding what you want from the relationship and listing out all the shortcomings from your partner. Couples should treat each other with respect and courtesy, and calmly express to each other what they need reconnect in their relationship rather than demanding it.

Partners aiming at reconnecting and building intimacy must develop strong listening skills. It is through intense listening that couples reach a full understanding of what his / her partner is saying and not saying. Listening to one's partner is not limited to just hearing what they say; for partners to really listen to what there significant other is expressing, they need to take not of other subtle ways of communicating such as hand gestures, body movements, and body language. These no verbal communications sometimes say more than what partners are willing to share with each other because of fear of judgment, criticism, or insecurities. Gently asking your partner to clarify on issues can help reach a better level of understanding and prevent misinterpretations; though more often than not, messages passed across in non verbal form are more truthful. To reconnect relationships, couples have to create a deeper level of understanding between them and this can only be done when they listen to each other. Listening to one's partner shows a sign of support and importance. It shows they have a high level of regard for each other and care about him / her thoughts and feelings. When couples feel like their partner care enough to listen to their thought and feelings, it stimulates the part of them that yearns for care and affection. They begin to feel at ease with each other and this propels them to share even deeper thoughts that makes them feel the most vulnerable. When couples reach that stage of reveling their vulnerability to each other, their emotional barriers are considerably lower than normal and in this state, relationships can be easily reconnected and emotional intimacy created.

Although working to reconnect relationships involves two willing participants, listening and understanding relationship expectations is entirety up to the partner to whom these feelings and thoughts are being expressed. The partner has to put aside his/ her own personal thoughts and feelings to understand his / her partner and vice versa.

While reconnecting, admitting to hearing and understanding your partner's expectations, fears and thoughts gives your partner the illusion of finally being seen. Simply saying "I understand what you are going through " shows your partner that you listened to him/ her, you relate with him / her, and you empathize.

When reconnecting partners fully understand each other, it clears away the doubts and fears in the relationship and also every ill feeling of misinterpretation and miscommunication. Reconnecting relationships helps partners understand each other better and see thing from a different perspective. This creates feelings of kindness, companion and empathy which is important in sustaining relationships.

Research has shown that building intimacy between partners requires asking mutual questions. A deep level of intimacy is achieved when partners in an emotional relationship asks and answers questions about their own perspective. Asking and answering questions gives one a deeper glance into the mind of one's partner; it helps one to understand why one's partner behave and think in a certain way. It helps partners to understand how each other think, act and feel about certain issues. When asked questions about childhood and growing up, individuals tend to drift into storytelling. Lost in the feelings reminiscing about fond childhood memories, it becomes easier for partners to share little amusing anecdotes about favorite childhood memories. In this state, one might learn his / her partner is a dare devil (for agreeing to do a dare to jump off the roof without a helmet) or has a fear of heights (which he/ she developed from sustaining a head injury after jumping off the roof). Such inconsequential details would bring a feeling of closeness between partners and this will strengthen their relationship.

Asking questions also helps one in choosing a suitable partner. Through casual conversation and asking questions, individuals could select the best possible partner for themselves; a partner with shared interests, similar expectations, and desirable behavioral traits to develop an intimate relationship with. Asking questions inspires conversations that can help emotionally distant partners reconnect their relationship in a non confrontation way.

The aim of this book is to guide partner on how to build and maintain intimacy and reconnect relationship using questions and conversations to inspire positive changes in the behavior and attitudes of partners towards each other and their relationship.

CHAPTER 1 :
WHO IS MY PARTNER?

As a result of Human's genetically programmed need for love and belonging, individuals at a certain point choose a partner to build a relationship with. Choosing a partner to build intimacy with involves a delicate process of selection and elimination. During this process, individuals compare possible candidates, and most often than not, make a decision based on compatibility and attraction. Compatibility in partners does not necessarily mean a perfect match. However, if both parties have a mutual sense of respect and equality, possess the same or similar goals, have a shared interest, and expectations that do not contrast against each other, share genuine companionship, and meet each others standard for a partner, an emotional connection could be formed between them.

Getting to know your partner is paramount in forming and maintaining an emotional connection. Couples cannot feel close, connected and intimate with one another without knowing each other. Knowing ones partner goes beyond having basic knowledge about what he/ she does for work, what zodiac sign he / she falls under, favorite color, or favorite food is. Although knowing those little details helps couples coexist better, it is not enough to create and sustain an intimate relationship between them. (Your next door neighbor can know all those things about you; it does not mean you have a close intimate relationship with them.)

Getting to know your partner helps you attain a deep understanding of how their mind work. Spending time with one's partner could be a good way but to know ones partner but asking questions and initiating intimate conversations have proven to be more effective. Communication is key in budding relationship because it gives the room for a back and forth flow and exchange of information which will help couples understand each other better and create intimacy between them. During the early stages of romance, couples tend to get carried away with the developing feelings they have towards each other and skip the "getting to know you" part of the relationship, jumping straight to commitment and cohabitation. Eventually, the thrill of new love gets dulled after couples settle into domesticity, then the realization that they are basically coexisting strangers hits. It is at this stage that issues begin to arise in the relationship because both partners do not know how to coexist in the same space because they do not really know each other. In order to reconnect, partners have to know each other to understand themselves better and avoid conflicts and disagreements.

When partners know each other, it creates an opportunity for transparency and trust to grow between them. There is a sense of closeness that comes with knowing each other which will provide the avenue for partners to share problems and confide in each other. This is accompanied by understanding which strengthens bonds between partners. Knowing your partner's expectations, strengths, weaknesses, fears and hopes will inspire a feeling of belonging. It helps ones to better understand the reason behind certain actions and prevent misinterpretations between partners.

Partners in a romantic relationship cannot hope to successfully cohabit together in the same space without basic knowledge of each other. To build and maintain a strong sense of intimacy and emotional connection which is important for the success of every relationship, partners need to have an insight to the minds of each other ie; how they think, what drives them, their secret guilty pleasure, how certain things make them feel, etc.

There are various important factors that shapes an individual's personality and influences his / her attitude toward relationships and formation of intimacy. Asking questions and conversations with the aim of knowing these underlying factors can help partners understand each other and build long lasting intimacy.

CHILDHOOD

Human beings are at their most vulnerable around people they care deeply for. This is usually the family and emotional partner; thus it is expected that emotional deficiencies in one relationship would affect or influence the other. The period of childhood is a long time spanning over a number of years. During this extended amount of time, deficiencies or irregularities in intimate relationship especially with one's primary care givers affects ones perception of emotional relationships greatly because it is in this period one's primary personalities are formed. These childhood experiences and events greatly influences an individual's need for attachment, love and support. The kind of relationships an individual had or witnessed during his/ her formative years is more likely to be adopted into adult relationships. This shapes their idea of what love is and it influences how they receive and give love. An individual who was neglected during childhood might develop a strong sense of self reliance and be reluctant to form any kind of emotional connection or intimacy. This is because the kind of habits and way of life an individual adopts during childhood form the basis of their personality, what they like, what they don't like, their expectations, etc. Such an individual would have the mentality of total independence and depend on his/ herself for the emotional needs one expects from a partner because he /she grew up to become emotionally closed, avoid any form of intimacy because of the fear of rejection, and is generally incapable of trusting anyone; which is necessary for creating and maintaining intimacy. Individuals either tries to adopts their parents type of love and relationship or strive to create the opposite of the kind of love to relationship he /she witnessed during childhood. Either way, their perception on love and relationships are built on the examples set by other people during Childhood and the type or absence of love during formative years.

The degree to which one's partner is willing to build intimacy or reconnect relationships is greatly influenced by their perception of what love is. For example, an individual from a family that is not openly affective could develop problems with his / her partner if him / her belives in constant show of affection. Without understanding each others childhood and how it affects their relationship, one partner would see the other as being needy and insecure while the other would see him/ her as being cold, distant and standoffish. Or an individual who experienced physical and emotional violence during childhood might think it is acceptable and normal to physically and emotionally assault their partner because that was their own reality during childhood and growing up years.

From an early age, individuals learn to adapt to whatever unit of family they fall into. This involves adopting certain behavioral traits from older members of the family which goes on to form the basis of one's personality. They learn to adopt certain behaviors that fits into their family dynamics and keep behaving the same way up to adulthood without any sense of self awareness, because those behavioral traits has become part of their self image. This could go both ways; an individual would either adopt certain behaviors from family members and try to project emotional relationships from childhood into adult relationships or yearn for the opposite of what he/she experienced during childhood.

Understanding why your partner acts a certain way, may mean understanding the kind of childhood he/she had. An individual might grow up to be extremely clingy and develop an irrationally fear of abandonment if he/she had emotionally selective care givers. The desire for love and a sense belonging not met during formative years, may cause the individual to develop an irrational fear of being neglected in the relationship, which may lead to them being overly possessive about everything that concerns their partner. In this same way, an individual with dismissive care givers might develop a sense of being unworthy of love, approval seeking and need constant affirmation of the fact from his/her partner which can be termed as needy. They tend to be people pleasers, putting the need of others before theirs to their own detriment, in the bid to buy affection. Individuals with overly compensating care givers might develop a sense of entitlement in adult relationships. They tend to have unrealistic expectations of their partners and when these impossible expectations are not met, they become frustrated and passively aggressive towards their partner which creates an emotional distance between them. Also, an individual with overbearing care givers might become overly dependent on his/her partner. In this situation, the individual leaves all the decision making and goal setting process to his/her partner because he/she has become accustomed to having those kinds of decisions made for him/her, thus projecting the childhood relationship with care givers into the adult relationship with one's partner. This leads to an unhealthy relationships, because at some point the partner being depended on will begin to feel overburdened with issues both partners are supposed to work on together. Individuals with overly involved care givers could also develop a weak sense of personal identity; enmeshment, where an individual do no know who they are aside from their personal relationships. They need to be constantly joined with another person to feel complete which will make them completely dependent on their partner. These emotional instabilities arising from early childhood experiences if not worked through, could prevent the formation and maintenance of a successful relationship. A successful relationship involves two equal adults with mutual love and respect working together to meet set goals in an atmosphere of loving companionship.

When partners get to know each other through asking questions and conversations, and understand each others childhood experiences and how it reflects on their current relationship, it makes it easier for them to settle differences because then they understand the underlying reason behind certain actions and attitudes and harmoniously work on then with the aim of rebuilding of and reconnecting relationship.

CULTURAL AND FAMILY TRADITIONS

Family traditions are important because it gives one a source of identity. It gives one an introspect into one's family history, origin, and tells one how certain events shaped family life. This instils confidence, comfort, and a sense of security and support in an individual to be part of something special that bonds a group of people together. Familial bonds are strengthened when families share sacred traditions and rituals. It creates a feeling of closeness and interdependence between them.

It is impossible to separate family traditions and cultural traditions. Family traditions are generally gotten from their cultural traditions. Individuals are made up of a crisscross of multiculture that forms our cultural identity. Culture manifests in many ways, through nationality, race, ethnic background, economic class, gender, political affiliation, socioeconomic philosophies, etc. Getting to know ones partner entails learning about his/her culture because it molds their way of life, how they think, how they dress, what they eat, their values and beliefs, etc. Culture goes beyond certain food, style of dressing, and music particular to a religious group. Culture is the entity that shapes beliefs, values, Ideologies and principles that guide day to day life. Understanding a person's culture gives a clear picture of what his/her life's philosophy and the reason behind it.

As far back as childhood, individuals are taught what is right and what is wrong according to societal norms and familial culture. This goes on to shape their views on life how they behave and how to relate with other people. This instilled way of life (culture) influences the formation of intimacy and sustaining relationships between partners; Cultural norms and values influences an individual's behaviors and attitude towards intimacy and relationships. For example, in a cultural setting that discourages open emotional communications, partners will find it difficult if not impossible to establish true intimacy with each other because their culture goes against open communication. This shows that the type of culture present in a relationship setting determines the level of communication between partners which influences the formation and maintenance of emotional intimacy between partners. It is only when partners understand each others culture and family traditions that they are able to understand and justify behaviors and reactions. Partners may be forced to learn each others culture and values in order to successfully cohabit together. This may not be easy because learning a new culture different from one's instilled culture may be strange and foreign concept which may result in a break in emotional connection and communication.

Partners from different cultural backgrounds does not necessarily mean they have different nationalities, ethnic groups or race. Because our philosophical views, values and beliefs makes up part of our culture, partners from the same country, the same race and the same ethnic group could still have different cultures. Exploring, understanding and appreciating each others culture would help partners respect each other differences and opinions and prevent them from drifting apart from each other due to cultural differences.

Navigating through cultural differences in a relationship requires a lot of compromise. Partners will have different opinions about certain issues due to cultural differences but must be willing to compromise to prevent conflict. Partners do not have to lose their own sense of identity ie; cultural traditions and adapt to a new culture in a bid to settle conflict. This would cause a load of identity which would lead to frustration and resentment. Rather, couples should search for a common ground between both cultures, common values, beliefs and interests between both cultures and compromise on issues, agreeing on a point that respects and agrees with both cultures.

Albeit an individual's culture influences his/her behavior, it does not entirely make up the basis of his/her personality. Asking questions and getting to know one's partner on a deeper personal level instead of making assumptions based on cultural stereotype helps to hasten the "getting to know each other " process. Cultural stereotyping can be misleading because there are certain parts of culture an individual might not adopt and when his/her partner assumes he/she is a particular type of person based on these cultural traits, it can lead them to form a wrong perception about the individual, create confusion, and lead to misunderstandings between them. For example, it is fair to presume a scientist is an atheist, because the account of creation by science and the account of creation by the bible are extremely contradictory to each other. However, the individual might have found a point of compromise between his/her faith and profession. But without asking questions and having an open conversation, one would just assume based on cultural dictates and norms.

Although cultural differences can cause an array of issues affecting the building of intimacy in a relationship, it can be safely navigated through asking questions to fuel understanding about other cultures, understanding support and an effective open communication channel.

VALUES AND BELIEFS

An absence of set values and beliefs can make an individual to behave irrationally and develop undesirable behavioral traits. Values are a collection of guiding principle used to modify ones personal conducts. An individual's values guide his/her behavioral pattern and help them understand the difference between right and wrong. It is a set of principles of right and wrong behavior and that standard by which life altering decisions are made. Values arises from one's socioeconomic status, religious and cultural backgrounds, family traditions, etc which shapes ones behaviors and personality.

To understand your partner's behavior and response to certain events, one need to understand his/her core values, which are guiding principles on the way life should be lived. Our values, beliefs and principles shapes ones perspective on life in general and how we relate with other on an intimate and interpersonal level.

Partners with the same values often share a similar views on the dictates of life. Individuals do not just develop these values overnight. The are instilled over time either by socioeconomic factors, family, religious and cultural dictates, etc. Partners with the same or similar values often share the same view on life. They believe in the same things and share a similar perspective on the world in general. This can strengthen their relationship and build intimacy between them because shared values and beliefs gives partners a sense of togetherness, separate from other people, because they both share the same perspective and views on how the world works. Shared values breed a feeling of intimacy between partners and helps them see things from the same perspective which strengthens their emotional bond. Shared values does not necessarily mean partners have identical behaviors, it simply means they have the same or similar views on behavioral modifiers like dependability, Spontaneity, commitment, loyalty, perseverance, efficiency, work ethic, open /closed mindedness, family life and traditions etc.

A person's values and beliefs builds his/her self identity. These values gives individuals a sense of self awareness, ("i am what I am, different from every other thing, because of what I believe in") and a general view about themselves and the world in which they live in. Values and beliefs makes up the totality of a person's worldview, what they make of the world around them, their expectations of the world, their place in it, etc.

It is important for partners to understand each others personal core values because they characterize behavior and influence the decision making process in day to do life. Understanding what values your partner posses helps to give reason to certain behavioral traits that couldn't otherwise be explained. For example, if your partner values kindness to strangers, it is normal to see him/her jumping to the aid of everyone in need, even to their own detriment because their values holds being kind in a high regard. This, it becomes part of their identity (he/she is a very kind person).

For partners to know each other, understand each other and build intimacy, it is important that they understand each others values and beliefs. It gives them an insight into the workings of each others minds, the basis of their personalities, and other entities that shape their world view, self identity, influences how they relate with other people on an intimate level. In order to build intimacy with one's partner and reconnect relationships, partners do not have to adopt each other's values and beliefs to create shared interests and goals, rather they should find a common interest, while retaining core personal values and compromise on issues arising from differences in values and beliefs.

PERSONALITIES AND BEHAVIORAL TRAITS

When partners know each other's behaviors and personality quirks, it becomes easier for them to understand the reasons behind actions and attitudes. The first step of building intimacy and reconnecting relationships is getting to know your partner. Although, people often say no one person can know another person completely, it is relatively easier to know your partner's behavior through asking questions, incitement open conversations and observation, and this knowledge can be used to predict actions to build intimacy between partners.

Astrologers believe that an individual's time of birth can be used to predict behavior and personality, however research carried out in the field of psychology states that human personality is made of five (5) basic traits which exists on a continuum between opposites. The five major traits are:

• Neuroticism; which is characterized by feelings of anxiety and volatility versus emotional stability and confidence.

• Conscientiousness; which is characterized by persistence and responsibility versus sloppiness and laziness.

• Agreeableness; which is characterized by friendliness and empathy versus hostility and insolence.

• Openness to experiences; which is characterized by creativity and curiosity versus intolerance and rigidity.

• Extroversion; which is characterized by assertiveness and urgency versus introversion and shyness.

Although behavioral traits and personalities are not entirely responsible for shaping ones life, it's strong influence is visible in important aspects of life like career choice, relationship with one's partner and other people, family life, lifestyle choices, etc. Research carried out in the early 1980's on the theory of personality shows that the five (5) basic traits that form personality stated above have a predictive association with one's love life. They postulated that individuals with neurotic behavioral traits are prone to experiencing negative emotions and are characterized by a constant state of restlessness and uneasiness. Neurotic individuals are always on the edge, looking for negativity in every aspects of their life and in the lives of those around them. Individuals with this trait tend to exhibit constant feelings of nervousness and apprehension over uncertain issues. Individuals with neurotic pattern of behavior might experience difficulty in forming intimacy and reconnecting with other people due to personality defects, in the same way, individuals with partners that portray characteristics of neurotic behavioral traits might experience difficulty in connecting and coexisting with them because neurotic individuals tend to spread their negativity into their partners. This behavioral trait if not understood by partners could cause partners to grow apart, causing a breakage in emotional connection.

Individuals with conscientious and agreeable behavioral traits exhibits high levels of satisfaction in their relationships. They are content to just sit back and let events play out as they will without doing anything to influence it. Partners of individuals with conscientious and agreeable behavioral traits might begin to feel like their partners are indifferent towards them and their feelings and are content to let the relationship turn out which ever it does. However, this may not be the case, but the individual has being conditioned by his/her behavioral trait to be content with present conditions and let another person take charge. This signifies a high level of interpersonal trust and low impulsion in these behavioral trait.

Individuals with openness to experiences are naturally curious and intuitive as the name implies. They are highly inquisitive, difficult to satisfy, posses a deep need to explore and discover new things.

Individuals with extroversion behavioral traits have strong definitive characters. They are more outgoing and socially adaptive than the average person. They are skilled at handling relationships and tend to be more happier and in touch with their environment. They also tend to lack long term commitment characteristics and are more suites to forming short term relationships. Extroverts blossoms other people, they are easily liked and connect well with other people.

Understanding these behavioral trait helps one in choosing a suitable partner, navigating through the relationship and forming long lasting emotional bonds. Contrary to popular belief, individuals do not change their personalities to better suit that of their partner as time goes on. Differences in personalities of couples in a committed relationship could be negotiated through compromise, however people tend to choose partners with similar personalities to theirs. This phenomenon is known as associative mating. In this context, individuals create emotional bonds with people with similar or the same personality trait as them. This however, does not guarantee the success of the relationship.

In the search for a suitable partner, individuals ought to choose emotionally stable and well adjusted people to form long lasting bonds with in lieu of individuals with the same personality trait.

Recognizing the different behavioral and personality trait helps partners to predict behaviors and adapt to which ever personality traits one's partner exhibits.

Note that; though individuals do not select the category of personality trait they fall under, can decide to improve on the less desirable parts of their personalities in order to be more open and connected to his/her partner in an effort to build intimacy and reconnect relationship.

INFLUENCES AND ROLE MODELS
An individual's role model has great effects on every aspect of his/her life. Role models influences ones views, values, personality, and actions. Role models are people an individual looks up to as exemplary figure deserving of honor, respect and admiration. Individuals yearn to be like their role models, they try to act, think, dress and even talk similar to

their role models because of the admiration they have for them and the desire to want to be like them. Role models serve as sources of inspiration for individuals, they help in motivating an individual to meet set goals and aspirations. Individuals often believe in their role model which in turn lead them to believing in themselves. For example, an individual aspiring to be a professional basketball player could have legendary basketball player Michael Jordan as a role model. His beliefs in Michael Jordan if infused with belief in his own ability as an athlete can build a strong sense of confidence in such an individual; role models gives individuals an insight into the struggles of others to reach their set goals and motivates them to do that same too, (if my role model can do this, I can do it too). Role models are very important because they can influence an individual's perspective of life in general and affect decision making process. Individuals, especially young adults and children because they are more impressionable easily develop role models from different areas. Role models could be developed from one's family, school, community, work place, mainstream media, etc. It is normal to see a child dressing up and acting like a comic book character because he/she admires that character and wants to be like that. In the same way, adults also pick role models from persons they wish to emulate and this role models serves as mentors and guide in negotiating day to day life. When individuals admire a person or group of people, they being to associate and identify with them. These role models could either be real people or fictional characters, but they help shape an individual's self identity and awareness.

Our first influences and role models as human beings are our parents. During childhood, individuals depend on their parents for everything ranging from emotional needs like love, support, stability, trust, encouragement, etc to basic needs like education, feeding, clothing, housing, etc. This build a feeling of loyalty and belonging between the child and his/her parents. Parents and primary care givers influences every aspects of life. During childhood, parents and care givers have the power to socialize an individual in any way they deem best, they instill their own ideologies and beliefs in the child which goes on to form the basis of behavior, attitude and perception about the world around them. The degree to which an individual was loved during childhood or the absence of it, is reflected in the individual's emotional availability and stability in adulthood.

Parents and care givers as first role models also influence an individual's perception on love and relationship issues. It is likely that partners would adopt their parent's relationship dynamics into their own because that is what they have been socialized into as the norm. For example, a woman from a family with strict gender specific roles who have been socialized into believing it is a woman's job to do certain tasks in the family, will adopt this same ideology with her partner. When met with resistance or her partner tries to help her, she might begin to feel slighted and see the offer for help as inadequacies on her part as a woman.

Much learnings that occurs in childhood are passed from parent and care givers to child through observation and imitation Without directly teaching an individual about love and relationships and giving instructions, parents and care givers still influences ones views on love and relationships through observation and emulation of the dynamics of their own relationship by their ward. While growing up, individuals tend to copy behaviors from other members of the family in order to fit in the family unit. If a family talked a certain way, the individual learns to talk the same way, etc. In the same way, there is a high tendency for children with parents who smoke ti either smoke or detest smoking. Individuals tend to copy all aspects of their parent's and care givers behaviors, both positive and negative ones. For example, an individual from a family with a strong intimacy, love and support between them will grow up and adopt the same closeness and intimacy with his/her own partner because that is how he/she has been socialized to understand how a relationship works while an individual from a family that experiences frequent acts of physical and emotional violence will most likely physically and emotionally assault his/her partner or be physically and emotionally assaulted by his/her partner.

It is important for partners to know the type of influences and role models they both had growing up, to better understand certain views and opinions one or both parties may have towards relationships and love.

The first step of building intimacy between partners is the getting to know each other process. This can be done through understanding who your partner is by looking at the different phenomena that shaped one's personality, views as a human being and perspective one has towards love and intimacy. Asking questions that inspires meaningful and open conversations is also a good way to build intimacy and reconnect relationships.

CHAPTER 2:
WHAT TYPE OF RELATIONSHIP DO WE HAVE?

One of the major causes of a lack of intimacy between partners is little or no communication between them. For the success of the relationship, there is a need for steady flow of information and effective communication between both parties concerning their feelings, thoughts, experiences and expectations from the relationship so they can understand each other better and work towards shared relationship goals. When partners know what they both want from the relationship and from each other, it becomes easier for them to satisfy these wants and settle disagreements between them. Research has shown that intimacy is quickly achieved by partners when they answer mutual questions. The goal of this is to enlighten both partners about each others views on issues to prevent them from simply assuming which can lead to coming to the wrong conclusions about one's partner and cause misunderstanding between partners. Involving in intimate conversations also helps partners to build a closer bond with each other. This introduces a sense of closeness between partners which is necessary to build intimacy. Partners who have drifted apart from each other too can be reconnected through asking questions and initiating meaningful conversations. Having intimate conversations through asking questions that enhances openness and vulnerability helps partners to work through underlying issues that cause the drift in their emotional connection and help them reconnect. In selecting a partner for a long lasting relationship, individuals need to choose emotionally stable and agreeable partners to build intimacy with, and the fastest more effective way to knowing whether a person is emotionally stable or not is through asking questions on their views, thoughts and experiences in love and relationships in a bid to decide compatibility with the potential partner. Also, partners that do not have previously existing intimacy in their relationship can build a strong emotional intimacy through asking questions and being open to each other through meaningful conversations.

Creating and maintaining intimacy in a relationship is a two person job. Both parties have to agree to work together to create and maintain intimacy for the success of the relationship between them. Asking questions to understand each others views on issues requires trust, openness and vulnerability. When partners do not trust each other, they will not be a will to freely ask and answer questions truthfully. Therefore, both partners need to be willing to create intimacy and reconnect their relationship through asking and answering questions to initiate conversations that brings them closer.

The aim of this book is to guide partners on building emotional intimacy in relationships and reconnecting relationships through asking questions and initiating meaningful effective conversations that helps them understand each other and introduces a sense of closeness between partners.

The questions asked helps partners to know each other's stand on issues affecting their relationship. It shows their opinion about issues, their experiences, their expectations, their hopes, fears and aspirations towards each other and their relationship to help them understand each other better. Below are a series of questions partners could ask themselves and mutually answer to help them understand each other better, build emotional intimacy between them and reconnect relationship.

In relationships, there is a need for expression of clear intent and clarification of status for both partners to know where they stand with each other. This is called defining the relationship. In defining the relationship, partners have to have an open clear discussion about the semantics of their relationship which includes definition of terms, status of the relationship, rules and boundaries stating what is private and what isn't, expectations and relationships goals. This leads to asking the "what are we? " question. It is important for both partners to be clear on the type of relationship they have to eliminate assumptions and misinterpretations between which would cause more harm than good in the long run. Asking the "what are we? " question require a level of transparency, vulnerability and confidence because it opens one up to the possibility of disappointment. Partners may not have the same expectations from the relationship or mutual feelings for each other and though it may be disappointing, it is important to know where they stand with each other and their relationship. For example, an individual might feel the need to attach a label to his/her relationship making it a more committed exclusive relationship, while his/her partner might not be in that same space emotionally. In this case, the relationship is on a pendulum and could swing both ways. Either partners could decide to take some time to get to know each other better by spending more time together and building a more stronger emotional connection with each other or they could move to terminate the relationship. Either way, the decision needs to be unanimous with both partners in agreement, especially if partners decide to stick together. Some might argue about the logic behind defining the relationship (saying "if it's not broken, why fix it?), this is to prevent misinterpretations and misunderstandings between partners. When the relationship is not defined, both parties believe whatever they want to about the relationship, they have different views and opinions about the same relationship because they are looking at it from two different perspectives which would lead to one or both partners having a false sense of security or insecurities about the relationship and his/her partner by extension. Contrary to the popular notion of ignorance is bliss, in this context, ignorance is ignorance.

Although defining the relationship does not in any way guarantee it's success, it is important for the creation of a healthy bond between partners. Defining the relationship and attaching labels to it, gives individuals a clear picture of what they are and what they are not. It clearly states the rules guiding the relationship, for example, it is against the rules and regarded as infidelity for partners in a committed exclusive relationship to see other people while partners in a noncommittal open relationship are encouraged to see other people apart from their primary partner.

Before partners ask the "what are we?" question, it is important that they have their own set expectations and goals. Knowing exactly what ones expects for the relationship will help to effectively communicate one's needs and expectations to his/her partner without any meanings getting lost in translation. It is important to be as straightforward and blunt as possible; your partner cannot give you what you want if he/she is not clear on what that is. Partners must be sure they are ready to take the relationship to the next level before attempting to clarify and label the relationship. Outside influences like peer pressure, pressure from family members, age factor and biological clock syndrome, etc might make an individual feel the need to take the relationship to the next level without being emotionally ready yet. This can cause a break in their budding emotional connection and take both partners to a level they are not ready for. Individuals need to be sure they are doing it for all the right reasons before attempting to define the relationship with their partner. Below are a few tips to asking the "what are we?" question and labelling the relationship.

• Be as blunt as possible, clearly stating all expectations and goals from the relationship.

• Approach the question in a conversational manner, ie; do not be demanding.

• Encourage your partner to share their own relationship expectations.

• Do not try to convince your partner to change their decision or manipulate their decision to match yours, it is unhealthy for a growing relationship.

• Do not try to look for hidden meanings and messages in your partner's decision especially when it does not match yours. Take everything at face value.

• If you and your partner have different relationship expectations or want different types of relationship, be clear on the next step. Ask, "what is next?" and agree on it.

Defining relationships and putting labels on them might be an awkward scary process, however, it gives partners a clear cut insight into their relationship and each other's expectation and leaves room for adjustments and improvements which helps in building healthy long lasting relationships.

WHAT KIND OF RELATIONSHIP DO WE HOPE TO HAVE?

After mutually asking and answering questions to know each other's stand and expectations from the relationship, partners need to unanimously decide and agree on the kind of relationship they hope to have and harmoniously work together to building it. These are their joint relationship goals and expectations. For example, if partners harmoniously decide they want a more committed exclusive relationship, they might decide to get married or if they decide to improve their communication skills, they might decide to go to couple's therapy together or if they decide to spend more time together by doing joint activities, they might decide to take a cooking class together or go hiking together etc. Deciding on an ideal relationship and working towards achieving it requires redefining of the previously existing relationship. Redefining the relationship involves modifying the already existing relationship to suit the emotional needs of both partners. This involves compromising and finding on a common ground and agreeing to look at the relationship from a new perspective. Both partners relationship expectations are taken into account and merged, creating a relationship ideal for both parties. Redefining a relationship entails rebuilding up the relationship from the foundation level, through compromise, love and support from both partners into the ideal relationship that meets the emotional needs of both partners and builds intimacy between them.

When partners expand the definition of their relationship, it leaves room for the creation and maintenance of emotional intimacy between them. In order for partners to successfully redefine their relationship and build a new healthier and stronger emotional connection and relationship with each other, there need to be an open line of communication between them. Knowing each others relationship and emotional expectations helps partners to rebuild their relationship into a better version suited to both partner's expectations. Knowing your partner's expectations is only possible through keen observation and effective communications between partners. When there is a free flow of information between partners, it becomes easy for them to meet each other's needs and expectations, explore new interests together, establish a pattern of interdependency and trust in each other and build and maintain intimacy.

In redefining and reconnecting relationships, it easy to assume that partners know what they need from each other, this can lead to conflict between partners if these needs are not met, not because him/her partner is incapable of meeting those needs, but because they do not know way those specific needs are therefore unable to satisfy inside them. order to rebuild a healthier, more stable, long lasting relationship, partners should effectively communicate their wants and needs to each other.

Redefining the relationship involves putting healthy boundaries in place, stating the rules, the do's and don't of the relationship to guild both partners on navigating through the relationship for its success. On this, both partners need to ask questions, have intimate enlightening conversations and agree on the specifics details of the relationship. For example, after asking the "what are we?" question, if the couple are on the same page emotionally and decide to move their relationship to the next level which may be being more committed to the relationship and to each other, the couple still have to decide whether the commitment comes with exclusivity or not. Partners have to be clear on every aspect of their relationship and avoid assumptions at all cost; one can never be sure what the other person is thinking without asking questions. In this case, if partners find out they have different views on their relationship (one person being committed and exclusive and the other being committed but not exclusive), it will create feelings of hurt, betrayal and disappointment between them which will lead to both partners being emotionally disconnected and potentially terminate the relationship.

The main ingredient for redefining relationship between connecting and reconnecting partners is open conversations and effective communication. While redefining the terms of agreement of the new and better relationship they hope to build, partners have to be emotionally open and vulnerable with each other, clearly stating their relationship expectations, needs, goals, thoughts and feelings in a friendly and conversational manner without pointing out each other's flaws and weaknesses to allow both partners empathize with each other and harmoniously work together for the success of the relationship. While stating what they want, partners have to try to be conversational, and not demand their expectations be met, but just simply state them and wait for their partner to respond. Research carried out on navigating relationships has shown that when partners push and demand for a change of status in the relationship, their partners are more likely to balk and push back than to give into their demands. For example, a woman demanding her partner proposes and move their relationship to the next level, if her partner is not on the same space emotionally yet and she keeps demanding and pushing for a ring, there is a high probability of the partner getting frustrated and terminating the relationship. In this state, partners should just be clear on their own expectations and give room for their partner to make his/her decisions on the previously mentioned expectations and communicate his/her own needs too. When this happens, partners should come together and agree on a point of compromise between, putting each themselves other's expectations into consideration and agreeing on a course of action or type of relationship that works best for both of them.

Therefore, in order to answer the "what type of relationship do we hope to have?" question, partners need to have clearly defined expectations and emotional needs, work together to realize these needs, and redefine their current relationship to better suit the emotional needs and expectations of both partners.

DOES PAST RELATIONSHIPS AND OUR RELATIONSHIP WITH OTHER PEOPLE INFLUENCE OUR EMOTIONAL NEEDS AND EXPECTATIONS?

Every person wants to be different; "the one and only ". They want to be the special one that arouses new unfamiliar feelings from their significant others, however to understand why partners act a certain way or why they have certain views and perspective of relationships, we need to take a look at past partners and previous relationships and relationships with people around them.

In our social world where relationships are formed on mutual interdependency, it is easy for one's relationships with other people to influence behavior, views and future relationships ie; the closer an individual gets to another person, the greater the possibility of influence. The ability to influence might not necessarily be deliberate, which makes it more effective. When individuals form close bonds with other people, especially emotional bonds, they tend to consciously or subconsciously modify their views to match those of the other person. These emotional bonds does not necessarily have to be romantic emotional bonds. For example, an individual with a fear of commitment and a close circle of happily married friends will eventually begin to rethink his/her commitment phobia and develop the need to be on the same level with the people around them. This is different from peer pressure because most times, the influencer does not know he/she is influencing the individual. Or an individual with openly affective parents might be influenced by his/her parents relationship dynamics and portray the same behavior towards his/her partner. Through assimilation, individuals in a close knit relationship pull each other into similar pattern of behavior, similar views and perspective on issues and similar relationship expectations without intending to.

Similarly, when partners in a relationship develop an emotional bond between them, they begin to lose their sense of singularity and see themselves as a single unit together As connection between both partners gets deeper, both partners self image begin to overlap and mix, and the lines between individuality gets blurred and partners start

43

adopting parts of each others personality traits. For example, a non athletic individual might engage in more sporting activities if his/her partner has vested interest in sporting activities. Or an individual's tastes in movies, music and even culinary preferences might be adjusted as a result of his/her partners influence.

Relationships helps to shape an individual's self identity by highlighting the desirable/ approved parts of an individuals personality and shunning or openly disapproving of undesirable parts of his/her personality. In every relationship, approved parts of personality is encouraged and these approved personality trait tend to stand out than the rest. When partners influences or adopt each other's personality traits, it either expands or shrinks their self identity. Self identity is the idea or image we have about ourselves. This is the perception and general view of how we see ourselves which encompasses our behavioral and personality traits, likes and dislikes, hobbies, vices, goals and aspirations. Basically, an individual's self identity answers the "who am I?" question. An individual's self identity is formed through a process of self discovery. In this process, individuals reach a better understanding of who they are as individuals and what is important to them.

However, in relationships one's self identity can be adjusted consciously or subconsciously by his/her partners influence. An individuals sense of self can either be expanded through development of new behavioral traits or shrunk to make undesirable behavioral traits inconspicuous. For example, a partner who smokes might give up smoking habits if it could be harmful to his/her partners health or an individual could modify his/her diet to match their partner's if their partner suffers from severe allergy to certain food substances. These examples are conscious influences one's partner can have, which inspires change in self identity. An individual's self identity can also be influenced subconsciously by his/her partner which would lead to a change in behavior, personality, perception and how they relate with other people. For example, if an individual whose self identity includes being funny has a partner that does not laugh at his/her jokes, such a individual's self identity will be adjusted; the individual would conclude that he/she must not be as funny as they thought which will change his/her self image, removing the sense of being funny from the list of qualities that makes up their self identity, causing it to shrink. In the same way, if the same partner always laughs at his/her jokes and agrees with the idea the individual has of his/her self as being funny, it will cause the personality trait to expand, causing the individual's self identity to be focused more that trait than others.

The types of relationship an individual has previously had also influences the level of commitment he/she is willing to form with a new partners and his/her expectations in the new relationship. Previous relationships sometimes determine how an individual treats his/her partner, the level of trust and openness he/she is willing to give, and the amount of work they are willing go give for the success of the relationship. An individual who is emotionally closed off to people around and has only being in non committed exclusive relationships will most likely be the same in a new relationship. As much as we want to be the different one; the ones that makes our partner feel something they have never felt before with anyone else, it is highly unlikely that individuals will change their pattern of behavior in a new relationship irrespective of their partners. The types of relationships had in the past strongly influences an individual's attitude in a new relationship. For example, it will be difficult for an individual who has had only non committal relationships to be openly expressive and committed in a new relationship and vice versa. Past partners also play a major role in modifying an individual's behaviors, reactions and nonreactions to experiences and events. For example, an individual that have had experience of infidelity with his/her previous partners will be more emotionally guarded and reluctant to build trust and Intimacy in a new relationship due to past events. In cases like this, partners can help each other work through these issues through reassurance and trust building activities.

Although it may be uncomfortable for partners to have conversations about previous relationships and past lovers, it is important in understanding certain behaviors, needs and expectations both partners have of each other. It could also help in predicting behaviors and reactions to certain events.

WHY DID PAST RELATIONSHIPS FAIL AND HOW DOES IT AFFECT PRESENT RELATIONSHIP?

As stated above, past relationships and partners may affect new relationships dynamics. Past partners and previous relationships affects or influences one's views, perspectives and emotional expectations of relationship even after said relationship has ended. In the same way, the method through which past relationship ended could affect ones new relationship and influence his/her relationship expectations. Past relationships carry more influence on new relationships depending on the type of relationship. For example, a divorced individual is more likely to be influenced by his/her past marriage than an individual that was not in a long term relationship with his/her former partner. This is because a stronger emotional bond was built over the course of the committed relationship than the emotional bond built during casual dating. Understanding past relationships of one's partner helps one to avoid situations and events that could potentially lead to termination of the relationship. For example, if an individual's previous relationship ended due to incessant complaining and nagging and his/her partner knew about it, it would help such an individual to modify his/her behavior to suit his/her partners needs and communicate without complaining about issues or nagging.

There are a lot of reasons why relationships fail. The major ones includes emotional and physical infidelity, disloyalty, lack of trust, understanding and empathy between partners, ineffective or lack of an open line of communication, emotional staleness, emotional and physical abuse, among many others. When partners in a committed exclusive relationship experiences one or more of the above reasons why relationships fail, it becomes difficult for the maintenance of such relationship. Experiencing one or more of the reasons listed does not necessarily mean there is no hope for the success of the relationship, but in order to rekindle feeling of affection and reconnect relationships, both partners need to agree and be willing to reconnect their relationship and put in the effort required for reconnection between partners.

Asking questions and initiating conversations about previous relationships can help partners understand each other better and help then to understand each others emotional and relationship expectations better. When redefining the relationship, partners may not have expressed their entire expectations from the relationship due to one reason or another, but individuals could find out exactly what their partner's relationship expectations are when asking questions about past relationships and why they failed. For example, while redefining the relationship and stating relationship expectations, an individual might not be able to share his/her need for attention to his/her partner for the fear of being called needy. However, during conversations about previous relationships and why they failed, such an individual might subconsciously confide in his/her partner on how he/she always felt ignored in past relationship which lead to disconnection between them and their past partners which ultimately lead to the termination of the relationship. In this case, an individual will then realize his/her partner's need to attention in the relationship and act accordingly for the success of the relationship.

Knowing the relationship history of one's partner also helps one to understand the negative traits of one's partner before attempting to build intimacy or reconnect relationships. An individual's history of past relationships acts as a blueprinted in predicting his/her behavior in regulating a new relationship. By understanding one's past relationships, an individual could gain insight into how his/her partner would behave in a new relationship. Human beings are naturally creatures of habit. It is highly unlikely that an individual's personality and habits could entirely transform to match his/her new partner's, therefore old habits in previous relationships can be used to predict behavior in a new relationship. For example, an individual that has a history of infidelity in past relationships will most likely be unfaithful in a new relationship too. Same goes for an individual who is emotionally and physically abusive, he/she will most likely portray the same abusive nature in a new relationship. Other individuals whose relationships ended as a result of addiction problems like addiction to recreational drugs, pornographic addiction, gambling addiction and alcoholism etc, will definitely portray the same addiction problems in a new relationship if such individuals have nor sought professional help. Knowing this helps individuals to decide if they still want to build intimacy or reconnect relationships with their partners.

Also, in the course of relationships, individual's behaviors and personality are modified either consciously or subconsciously. An individual's partner has the ability to influence and alter his/her partner's personality and behavioral traits to better suit their own, which may in some cases, lead to acquiring peculiar personality traits. In this context, knowing and understanding such an individual's past relationships will help partners understand each other better which will create an avenue for creating intimacy. For example, an individual that has had a close relationship with a germophobic (an extreme fear of germs and obsession with cleanliness) partner, might have subconscious adopted some behavioral traits/ quirks from his/her past relationship which will be better understood when his/her new partner knowledge of the past relationship.

Thus, asking questions and initiating conversations with the aim of understanding why past relationships failed, what they entailed and how they affect individuals attitudes towards new relationships helps partners understand each other better, which could build a stronger emotional bond between them and create intimacy.

DO WE HAVE RESIDUAL FEELINGS FROM PREVIOUS RELATIONSHIPS AND HOW DOES IT AFFECT PRESENT RELATIONSHIP?

In the same way that past partners and previous relationships can influence new relationships, behaviors and attitude towards the new relationship, holding on to residual feelings from previous relationships also affects new relationships. These residual feelings could either be positive feelings or negative feelings towards an individual's past partner and relationship. Positive residual feelings towards ones previous partner could be in form of leftover feelings of love, affection, admiration, physical attraction, etc. It is normal to still care about a person one once shared a deep connection and emotional bond with, however if after the termination of such feelings, and these emotions of affection, love and physical attraction still linger and the individual enters a new relationship with a different partner, it may be difficult if not highly unlikely for such an individual to form a deep connection or an emotional bond with his/her new partner. Negative residual feelings towards ones previous partner and relationship could be in form of anger, and resentment. Resentment between partners is caused by underlying issues of guilt, anger and the unwillingness of partners to forgive each other. Negative feelings and resentment grows in place of love and affection when partners keep scores of past fights, hold grudges against each other and purposely seek to cause intentional hurt through hurtful words and actions.

Resentment is built over time; it rises up from a series of annoyances and peeves which continually grows if not dealt with. Partners that resent each other slowly looses all feelings of affection and kindness they have for each other and slowly become passively aggressive towards each other. This happens in a slow and gradual process that partners might not even notice till said resentment have destroyed the relationship.

Although relationships can be terminated for a number of reasons, it is possible for individuals to develop feelings of resentment towards previous partners over the way their relationship ended. For example, if a committed exclusive relationship ended as result of infidelity and a long history of lies to cover up one's tracks, it is almost given that the partner being cheated on will develop feelings of resentment amongst other negative feelings towards the unfaithful partner. In cases like this, even after the relationship has ended, individuals tend to hold on to those feelings of hurt and betrayal and use them either as a yardstick to judge new partners by or as an instrument of protection to guard them from being hurt like that again. Either way, holding on to resentment or any form of negative feelings from previous relationships affects or influences one's new relationship. For example, if one partner in a relationship still has positive residual feelings like love, affection and physical attraction for his/her previous partner, such an individual would not feel the sense of closeness and emotional connection with his/her new partner which is necessary to build intimacy between them. The individual may not even feel the need to develop any type of closeness or emotional intimacy with his/her new partner because he/she is still emotional attached to the previous partner. This would create an emotional distance between the individual and his/her partner and cause the partner to begin to feel neglected and unwanted. This could also cause the individual's partner to develop feelings of resentment towards him/her if the individual's partner has already formed an emotional attachment to the individual and such feelings were not reciprocated because of the individual's preoccupation with his/her previous partner.

Having negative residual feelings from previous relationships may lead to an individual developing unhealthy personality traits which may be prevent the creation and maintenance of emotional intimacy between partners in a new relationship. An individual that went through a bad break up or divorce (if previous relationship was marriage) from his/her partner and is still harboring negative feelings and resentment towards his/her previous partner might project insecurities from previous relationship into the new relationship and make unhealthy comparisons between past and present partners. These negative feelings could also lead to generalization of

characters (stereotyping) and holding new partner accountable for the shortcomings of previous partner because they share some characteristics like gender, nationality, career choice, etc. For example, it is common to hear people say that professional athletes are highly promiscuous; such infamous theory however could cause an individual whose partner is a professional athlete to be reluctant to trust and form deep connection with him/her because of personality trait society has attached to his/her career choice irrespective of who the individual is. Likewise, an individual still holding on to negative feelings towards his/her previous partner may not be able to completely be open with his/her new partner because of fear of being hurt again. However, this unfair to his/her new partner because it eliminates every chance of deep emotional connection between them and dooms the relationship they are trying to build from the start because an individual who is still holding on to negative emotions from past relationships will be emotionally unavailable to build intimacy and form deep emotional connections required for the success of the relationship. It is necessary for persons who have been hurt or betrayed in past relationships to try to forgive previous partners and let go of every negative emotions before starting a new relationship to avoid projecting old issues on a new slate.

It is also important for partners to be clear on whether or not they have residual feelings, either negative or positive from previous relationships in order for them understand each other better and to work through these feelings (or lack thereof) together.

CHAPTER 3 :
HOW DO WE RELATE WITH EACH OTHER?

Creating and maintaining relationships comes easy for partners that have a good relation with each other. When partners genuinely enjoy being in the same space, conversing, communing with each other and coexisting with each other, their relationship becomes effortless and smooth. This also gives them a better understanding of each others behavioral traits and quirks which helps them in predicting each other's behaviors, helps them to understand why one's partner behaves a certain way and guide them in acting accordingly.

Relationships with partners that are existing on the same wavelength and in total sync with each other are more likely to be long lasting and successful than relationships with partners that do not have a strong sense of relation between them. Being in sync with one's partner aids effective communications as partners who are in sync with each other are able to understand both spoken and unspoken messages being passed across through body language. When partners do not relate with other people properly, it is easy for partners to be oblivious to each others sufferings and problems if they are not verbally shared. This could cause an individual to feel lonely even in the relationship and become emotionally distant from his/her partner.

In order for partners to build emotional intimacy and reconnect their relationship, partners need to examine their level of relation with each other, and ask questions and have intimate enlightening conversations on how to deepen their relation with each other.

With the aim of building emotional intimacy and reconnecting relationship, partners have to find a means of relating better with each other. In order to partners to build intimacy there is a need for a sense of closeness and interdependence between them which can only be built when partners relate on a deeper level together. To reach this level, partners need to ask questions about what drives them, where they feel the most safety, their history and experiences, and other factors that makes him/her uniquely different from every other existing human being. Every human has different vibes to them, different ways to get comfortable. Some feel much relaxed and open only when they outdoors and one with mother nature's gifts. Some people feel more of themselves when they listen to music and/or other forms of art. Its just a matter of finding the 'it' for them. You may find that they talk about that specific thing a lot, they like to be around it a lot, or it brings certain level of peace, enthusiasm whenever they are around it. Creating better relations with one's partner is a two way street; both partners have to be willing to deepen the level of connection and communication between them to enhance a deeper level of intimacy and emotional connection between them. Notwithstanding, there are certain gestures that goes a long way in getting your partner to relate and connect better.

USING POSITIVE AND MOTIVATION WORDS DURING CONVERSATIONS.

When we use positive words on our partners and ultimately those around us, it tends to bring out their best sides, it makes them feel progressive and valuable. This can go a long way in ensuring a stable relationship. Even when faced with challenges from work place, societal pressure, it is really important that they believe there's someone who would always believe in them despite. As the saying goes "*positive vibes, can only yield positive fruits*".

• *Endearing nicknames /pet names*

Adults have found this to be very effective. Using nicknames for yourselves can help bring out the 'child-like' instincts in all of us. It makes them feel young again, playful, attractive, less tensed and special.

• *Having shared memories and experiences*

This involves planning and actually doing things together, going on vacations, planning special treats and dates for just you both, doing silly but less dangerous pranks on each other, video blogs, e.t.c. owning something together gets the bonding hormones flowing.

• *Respecting individuals point of view and opinions*

Whenever arguments arise, be it serious or not, its always important to try to understand their side of the story. Trying to prove difficult will only give the impression that you are more apart and will hardly find a common ground. This is really discouraging for any relationship even if the love started out strong. Ordinary arguments and disagreements can build up over time.

• *Thoughtful gestures like giving surprising and unnecessary gifts*

The act of gift giving has been the most effective way of showing your loved ones that they matter and that they are special. It is really important not to underestimate the simple gesture of giving, more so, if it's a thoughtful gift, something they have always dreamt of having, something they love and even surprising them with newer packages can be a way of opening their hearts.

HOW DO YOU KEEP CONNECTED AND IN SYNC WITH EACH OTHER?

All relationships require efforts, commitment, patience to stay alive and work. It is easy to drift apart and lose the emotional connection between them when partners get too comfortable with each other and stop trying to keep the emotional connection intact. In order for partners to stay emotional connection even when they are physically apart, there need to be a level of trust and emotional security between partners that allows them to rest easy even when they are thousands of miles away from each other. When partners have complete sense of closeness, belonging and togetherness, it helps them feel secured in their emotional connection with each other, because then they know that no matter what happens, his/her is on the same team with them. Different partners have different relationship dynamics. Ie; what works for Mr A in his relationship might not work for Mr B in his own relationship. This is a result of individual and behavioral differences. Thus, different individuals in different relationships have different ways of staying in sync with his/her partner, based on their behaviors/personalities and the type of relationship they have. Partners can be informed on how best to stay on sync with each other through asking questions and initiating intimate conversations. However, there are general universal tips that can be used to maintain sync between partners.

Here are some useful tips;

• *Spend quality time with your partner*

Planning and spending some time alone with your partner on a regular basis will help you both stay connected and feel special because quite often, as time goes, by we get entangled by work, raising a family and social duties and so we forget that it's important to keep the spark alive. You need yourselves of all the fun things you both did before all the extra curricula activities came into play. Sitting face to face and in close proximity to your partner on a regular basis can help bring solace.

• *Keep physical intimacy alive*

Touch comes with a power of affection, closure, trust, sensitivity. Frequent sex, touching, kissing, hugging, holding of hands can be a very effective way of staying connected to your partner. Affectionate contact boosts the body's levels of oxytocin, a hormone that influences bonding and attachment.

• *Stay communicated*

Whether short or long distance relationships, all requires adequate communications because communication makes your partner important, it keeps them updated on what you going through at every point in time and it's very difficult to get back on track once the bridge in communication is broken and left unattended to. This is the most vital part of every relationship. Make it a habit of telling your partner what you going through and not making them guess.

According to Lawrence Robinson, "*if you have known each other for a while, you may assume that your partner has a pretty good idea of what you are thinking and what you need. However, your partner is not a mind reader. While your partner may have some idea, it is much healthier to express your needs directly to avoid any confusion. Your partner may sense something, but it might not be what you need. What more, people change, and what you needed and wanted five years ago, for example, may be different now. So instead of letting resentment, misunderstanding, or anger grow when your partner continually gets it wrong, get in the habit of telling them exactly what you need*".

• *Give and take*

Relationship is a give and take business. When you recognize what important to your partner, it brings wholeness to him/her, it shows a measure of goodwill, thoughtfulness and a sense of devotion. On the other hand, it is also important for your partner to recognize your wants and for you to state them clearly. Constantly giving to others at the expense of your own needs will only build resentment and anger

HOW DEEP IS OUR EMOTIONAL CONNECTION?

In romantic relationships, the level of emotional depth and dependency between both partners determines the strength of that relationship. Communicating with your partner does not guarantee that you do understand what he/she is going through and often, partners may feel like their significant other listens out of sense of duty, not because they genuinely care or feel the way they do which could lead to him/her feeling small and insignificant. Emotional depth is being able to listen, interpret, sensitively respond to feelings that arises in your partner, others around you and ultimately yourself. This is ability to show empathy, to 'feel into' someone else's experiences to know what it feels like to be them. That level of interdependency gives both partners a sense of reliability, true friendship and a deep intimate connection that is built over time. This, as well as empathy takes time to become insoluble, because there are significant factors that affects the level of transparency and vulnerability needed between partners to achieve desired emotional depth and intimacy. We often want our partner to be able to talk to us about everything and also to be the first person they think of sharing their emotions with whenever they going through something be it Positive or Negative but we also have to understand that no human being was ready made as certain factors such as early/childhood environmental factors, prominent life changing experience and events, gender and gender roles as dictated by society, and an individual's background and culture can affect and influence an individual's perception and personality which in turn dictates the individual's ability to understand, empathize and form emotional connections with his/her partner.

• *Early/Childhood environmental factors*

Undoubtedly, this forms the base of any character, personality and behavioral traits of all creatures. During formative years, specific behavioral traits are instilled in individuals depending on the kind of family (on a smaller scale) and society (on a larger scale) an individual is born into. Families and society at large go on to shape an individual's perception of love and affection amongst many other things. Individuals while growing up, adopt their families and society stipulated method of showing love and affection. Therefore, If your partner grew up in an emotionally responsive environment, where feelings are being shared/opened up, ideas are welcomed, personal identities are recognized and welcomed, chances that you will struggle with emotional connections with your partner are quite low. However, if their childhood memories were ones filled with condemnations whenever emotions were expressed, traumas, personal opinions weren't welcomed, felt invincible by those around them, to survive, they tend to generate a responsive character to against such phenomena's. These are often putting up firewalls against everyone in their adult years, self-reliance, hardly feeling the need to need anyone else but themselves, anger, because they grew up fighting to be heard. It takes a lot to bring all these to awareness, to get them to recognize these behavioral and personality traits and ultimately overcome them.

• *Prominent life changing events and experiences*

It has been said that every individual is a sum of his/her experiences. Our experiences contributes to our self identity, perception of the world, our values, views, thoughts, fears, expectations, etc. However, some experiences and events stand out more than others because of the effect and influence they have on an individual's identity, behavior/personality and his/her life in general. These experiences are known as defining moments and they are often not recognized when in motion, only after the moments are passed are the impacts of such experiences realized.

An individual's defining experiences can strongly influences his/her ability to form and maintain emotional connections with relationship partners and other members of society. For example, if an individual has had defining experiences, probably during childhood and formative years, where he/she is rejected by his/her family and his/her need for belonging neglected, such an individual may be unable to form and maintain emotional connections during adulthood and in romantic relationships.

• *Gender and gender specific roles*

The laws of society dictates that women are nature's caretakers. They often extend their emotional tables as that's their primal designs. This can cause an upside as they can sometimes not be taken serious. They appear weak and vulnerable and opportunists can take that and devalue it. They often do the "emotional labor" of both themselves and their partners. This overfunctioning is a product of a patriarchal social system in which emotional intelligence, considered a female quality, is simultaneously devalued and overly demanded from others.

Men have the general idea that being emotionally vulnerable makes them a weaker primate. They are taught to express only anger and dominance if they are ever going to get the good stuffs, so every other feeling are suppressed. Showing strength solidifies their role in the society and thus they tend to see that as the solution to every problem. This means that, they understand feelings of others less.

• *Background/Culture*

When there's a cultural difference between couples, difference in norms, beliefs, cultural origins and flair, this often cause disparages between them. An individual's culture encompasses his/her way of life, which includes practice that one grows up with, seeing others as invaluable, impertinent or less important. For some, their culture and practice is non-negotiable and whoever wants to get involved with them have to by all means follow suit. For them, their entire existence is intertwined with their practice and their emotional connections capabilities are dictated within the do's and don't of their culture and cultural backgrounds.

For the success of every relationship, there need to be a strong emotional connection between both partners. Not only emotionally, partners need to build a strong connection emotionally, intellectually, spiritually, etc in order to build intimacy between them.

IS MY PARTNER EMPHATIC TOWARDS MY FEELINGS?
If one's partner is not sensitive enough, they might find it difficult to express absolute emotions towards the other. They are less familiar with the act of absorbing people's emotions or physical symptoms. They filter the world through logics and facts. The trademark of an empath is feeling and absorbing other people's emotions. Displaying this attribute would require a selfless attitude and an understanding that not everyone thinks and feels the same way. However, this can be overemphasized in a relationship and can become the very problem. Couples needs to have a deeper understanding of each other, be intuitive, scale your partner thoroughly, and understand when he/she needs an alone time, wants to be heard, wants to listen, what thigs matters to them and be sure let them know what matters to you as well. When emotions are communicated through words, signs, touch, couples would assume a deeper emotional stance between each other.

If you want your partner to be emphatic towards your feelings, you have to be able to give back the same. As Tony Robbins says, "a relationship is not a place *you go to get, it is a place you go to give*". You may not want to wait for them to make the first move, because as stated earlier, your partner may not know the 'how' on showing empathy. So leaving it to them may not be the best decision if one is thinking of reconnecting one's relationship back to its blooming ways. There's a chance that your partner may still not respond positively to any and all gestures made to resuscitate the relationship but you can't affirmatively tackle the situation if you don't know from where the problem stems from. What's not making them pay attention. What is it they need. What is most important to you both. Is your relationship on the scale of importance for you both? What are you both getting out of this. Why would you want to do this all over again? Part of statements afflicted couples give in therapy is "he/she always puts their needs first", "he/she always wants me to come forward first before we deal with our issues", "he/she is selfish". Ultimately, it's important to take responsibility of our own needs, as that's the whole point to being an adult. However, if couples recognize that part of what's required in being someone else's significant other is taking their own needs as equally important as well.

DOES MY PARTNER WEIGH HEAVIER ON THE EMOTIONAL INTIMACY SCALE?

Emotional intimacy mentioned been the solid earth on which the foundation of every relationship sits unto. **Psychology Today** describes Emotional Intimacy as "closeness that requires *a high level of transparency and openness. This involves a degree of vulnerability that can feel uncomfortable or anxiety-producing to many of us*". Without emotional intimacy, relationships risk eventual discord or brokenness even despite physical intimacy or weightless communications. Achieving the skill of balancing expression and containment of emotions as at when due requires one to consciously be aware of oneself and ones partner as well. Emotional intimacy allows one to share personal feelings, display caring attitudes, understanding, anticipating of feelings from those around you.

According to Wikipedia; The Emotional Intimacy Scale (EIS) is a scale which enables to evaluate the emotional intimacy in a relationship. Its goal is to predict the different outcomes produced by the existence of an intimate relationship. This scale is created with a study of different items which are fundamental components of an intimate relationship. Some persons need to answer to judge the degree of truth of each of these components in comparison with their actual situation. There are five of them:

• This person completely accepts me as I am

• I can openly share my deepest thoughts and feelings with this person

• This person cares deeply for me

• This person would willingly help me in any way

• My thoughts and feelings are understood and affirmed by this person

These results are put in correlation with specific values which characterize an individual such as psychological and physical well-being, social support and health.

The results provided by the scale prove a positive relationship between an increase of EIS and an increase for the individual of social support, self-efficiency, life satisfaction and other positive effects. It also shows the negative relation between a decrease of EIS and an increase of stress, pain, and fatigue for the individual. An intimate relationship gives a sentiment of purpose and belonging which increases the physiological and psychological well-being.

Essentially, there are three variables vital to Emotional Intimacy, albeit, these variables can be tricky, are not entirely dependent on each other, neither are they absolutes as we all experience intimacy differently. They are thus;

- Communication

- Romance, love, sex

- Vulnerability

- *Communication*

As essential as communication is, it isn't dependent on Time factor. Communication may not necessarily grow as time goes by. A couple that have been together for long can have communication problems if they have no shared experiences. It also does not surround talking about domestic duties, work, kids, family, money and businesses or couple of shared events with friends and family. It requires total transparency, vulnerability to survive and thrive.

- *Romance, Love, Sex*

Physical connections between couples gives a feel of convergence, passion, transparency, vulnerability, and ultimately agreement. This potent mix can give a satisfying and comfortable feel for both individuals participating in the relationship. Some see sexual intimacy as a core emotion, a deep and profound level of trust needs to be attained first.

- *Vulnerability*

Being vulnerable can be a scary thing as you are in a state where you are exposed, transparent. Research carried out in the field of psychology has shown that, the vulnerability involved in emotional intimacy is anxiety-producing to many. In this trench, Time can be a very important factor as trust can be built over time. As stated earlier, vulnerability from our partner is dependent on many variables. We may find ourselves in relationships where our significant other feels comfortable revealing less, withholds important information's about themselves and their past thus creating poor and unstable connection. We may also be paired with a partner who doesn't provide the confidence that we want or need, much less the acceptance of ours. The resulting void is a lack of intimacy that is often the impetus for an emotional affair, and thus in return, may lead to infidelity.

CHAPTER 4:
WHAT ARE MY PERSONAL GOALS?

Goals are aims and objectives an individual strives to achieve. Ones goals direct the path ones life take; every life altering and life shaping decisions are taken with one's goals and aspirations in mind. In the "getting to know each other " process, partners ought to ask questions about each others goals and objectives because it gives individuals an insight into the kind of life an individual wishes to live. Goals, aspirations and objectives are more than just career choices; although ones goals may include career choices, in relationships context, it is mainly focused on lifestyle and lifestyle choices.

In the same way that an individual's family and society they belong to influences behaviors and personality traits, ones family and society they belong to also influence their goals and aspirations. For example, an individual who experienced lots of hardship during childhood due to the low financial capabilities of his/her family might aspire to be wealthy so his/her own children do not have to go through the same hardship as they did. In the context of relationship, an individual that did not experience any feeling of affection either from his/her parents or between them, may be determined be different from what he/she experienced during formative years and strive to create intimacy and deep emotional connection between his/her self and their partner. Likewise, an individual who has previously experienced hurt and betrayal from emotional relationships can it his/her goal to remain emotionally unattached in future relationships.

An individual's short term goals and long term goals can be used to determine certain aspects the individual's personality. Short term goals as the name implies are goals and aspirations that cover a short span of time. These goals are easily attainable and in most cases, do not require a lot of effort. An individual's short term goals cover mundane areas of the individual's life. Long term goals are attained through reached through short term goals. These usually take years to reach and when they are realized, incite mien changes in an individual's life.

Our goals and aspirations is like a blueprint of how we want our life to go. It includes everything we hope to achieve in an entire lifetime. An individual's goals and aspirations also encompasses his/her relationship hopes and aspirations. When partners understand each other relationship goals, it gives them an insight into what his/her partner hopes to achieve in the course of the relationship, whether he/she hopes to build intimacy or not, whether he/she yearns for true emotional or not, it shows what partners are willing to give in a relationship and what they hope to get in return; their aims and objectives in its truest form.

An individual's relationship goals is different from his/her relationship expectations in the sense that, relationship expectations are what one hopes to get from their significant other and the relationship while relationship goals are aims and objectives an individual works towards in the course of the relationship. An individual's relationship expectations are either met or not by his/her partner; the individual has no power over this, while his/her relationship goals is solely up to them.

While building relationships, it is important for partners to know and understand each others relationship goals in order for them to know each others aims and objectives and what he/she hopes to achieve in the course of the relationship.

DO WE HAVE SHARED INTERESTS AND GOALS?

It is important for partners to have common goals and interests in a relationship. When partners share common interest, it reduces the probability of conflicts and disagreements between them and deepens their sense of closeness, intimacy an emotional connection. It is healthy for partners in a committed exclusive relationship to have some personal interests of their own in the relationship so as not to lose their self identity (unique characteristic and qualities that makes them who they are) but when partners get carried away with their individual interests and do not share any same interest as a couple, it decreases the amount of time they spend in each others space and eventually, partners will begin to feel disconnected from the relationship and also from each other. When partners have shared or similar interests, it widens their conversational areas and creates a more relaxed environment for partners to converse. With this ease in communication between partners, partners are able to get to know each other better, more willing to share deeply personal details about themselves with each other which leads to an open avenue for the creation of intimacy and a deeper level of emotional connection between them.

Partners with similar goals and interests can understand each other better that partners without similar goals and interests, because they are experiencing the same or similar events, so it becomes easier for them to understand and empathize with each other. For example, partners with the same career paths will be understand better and be in a position to offer professional advice when one partner is facing work related difficulties.

Shared interests and goals between partners is not a prerequisite or a guarantee for a successful long lasting relationship, however when partners share certain intrests, it becomes easier for them to understand each other, communicate better, quickly build intimacy between them and truly enjoy each others company. Partners in an effort to build intimacy and emotional closeness and connection might begin to feel obligated to spend time with each other, however if said partners have similar interests, it will cause both partners to be more relaxed and willing to spend time together because they will both be doing what they enjoy. Some of these interests might include sport preferences, hobbies, similar interests in movies/music etc.

DO WE HAVE CONFLICTING PERSONAL INTERESTS AND GOALS?
Conflict of interest arises in relationships when partners have personal goals and interests that work against each other. These contradicting personal goals may either be in form of major lifestyle choices like

whether or not they want children, different views on relationship type, different views on life, etc.

It is healthy for partners to have some different personal interests and goals outside of their relationship to maintain their self identity, however when there are no common grounds for them to meet, their relationship may begin to go on a downward spiral. An individual's life goals set the course for his/her life. Every major and minor decisions are taken with one's goals in mind, thus when partners personal goals contradict each other, it becomes almost impossible for then to harmoniously coexist in a shared space. In order for partners to peacefully coexist together, there is a need for a common ground between them where they both share the same perspective on relationships and life in general. When partners want similar things, meeting the emotional and relationship needs and expectations of each other becomes easy for them; it becomes like a give and take situation (you give your partner exactly what you expect to receive).

Partners who do not have similar or shared interests and goals could develop new interests together in a bid to build intimacy between them by having shared interests and spending more time together, partners could sit and decide on areas of shared interests they could equally enjoy. This is creating a common ground for both partners to harmoniously coexist on, in an effort for both partners to retain their self identity (and perhaps expanding it to contain new shared interests with one's partner) and develop shared interests with each other. Developing shared interest and goals does not mean adopting one's partner's own goals and interests. Developing new shared interests between partners should be a mutually new interests for both partners in order for them to experience these new interests at the same time.

It is normal to want to share your what you are passionate about with your partner and want him/her to feel as strongly about those interests as you do, however this may come across to your partner as you trying to change who they are to fit your own idea of who you think they should be.

Regardless how much partners try to create shared interests and goals by compromising and creating new interests and goals together, there are certain interests and goals that cannot be compromised on. For example, if partners have different views of their relationship and the roles they each play in it(ie; if one partner believes in gender specific roles where the female partner's job is creating a home and the male partner is charged with provision and protection and the other partner is against this idea has career plans of her own), this could cause disparities between partners which can only be solved when one partner gives up his/her views of how he/she thinks the relationship should be. Also, if partners have different views on whether or not they want children, this would put them on opposing sides and may even be a deal breaker for partners. If one partner wants to focus on his/her career and is of the opinion that children will change the entire dynamics of their relationship and the other partner wants to build a family together with children in the mix, such partners have contradicting goals. Compromising on such important goals may cause partners to resent each other as time goes on. In this context, the partner who compromised and opted out of having children because his/her partner was not in agreement with having children, may on time begin to feel like his/her partner is responsible for him/her not having the type of family he/she craves. Or the partner who compromised and had children to please his/her partner may later on begin to feel like his/her partner and the children they now share are responsible for limitations in achieving certain career goals. Assigning blame on each other for situations which in truth they may or may not have contributed to creates an emotional distance between partners. When partners hold each other relationship for unmet goals and aspirations, they may begin to feel like the only way to realize these goals is to break free and terminate the relationship.

It is important for individuals seeking to from an emotional connection and build a long lasting relationship to know that although having shared interests and goals could help foster feelings of affection, closeness and intimacy between partners, it is not a guarantee for a successful relationship. Partners also need to understand that setting common goals and shared interests in a relationship could help them reconnect by spending more time together. Also, when there are no common interest between partners in a relationship and partners compromise their own personal goals (which makes up part of their self identity) to accommodate their partner's own goals and aspirations, it could lead to feelings of resentment and regrets in the future.

Individuals seeking to build long lasting relationship need to ask questions and initiating intimate conversations about each others goals, aspirations and interests to make sure their personal goals and aspirations even if they are not similar, at least do not contradict each other.

CHAPTER 5 :
WHY DO WE DISAGREE?

Disagreements and arguments among couples are inevitable in a relationship. Because no two persons cannot be entirely identical in behavior no matter the common interests and shared goals, it is unrealistic to expect partners to coexist without conflict; partners are bound to have different opinions and disagree on issues both in their relationships and outside their relationship.

It is easy for partners to fall into a reoccurring pattern of conflicts and disagreements when they do not fully understand each others behavior and personality. This does not mean their relationship is flawed, it simply shows that in order for partners to reduce the rate of arguments, disagreements and conflict between, partners have to try to understand and empathize with each other

There is an infinite number of causes for disagreements in relationships ranging from major reasons like incompatibility in partners behavior, parenting methods, communication methods, finances, etc. But there are generally specific reasons why partners engage in conflicts and disagreements with each other. Understanding these reasons helps both partners to understand why his/her partner behaves a certain way or react to certain behaviors and why it results in conflict and disagreements. Some of these issues are:

• *unrealistic expectations and demands.*

When partners relationship expectations and needs are not met, they tend to become grumpy, frustrated, angry,

dissatisfaction , unhappy and may even develop feelings of resentment towards his/her partner. These negative feelings may affect the individual's relation with his partner, making him/her sarcastic and offhand towards their partner.

It is expected that partners in relationships have certain expectations from each other, but in order for this expectations to be met, partners have to clearly state them. It is unreasonable to keep mute about one's expectations and needs from the relationship an expect such needs to be addressed. Although partners with deep connection between them could communicate through body languages, relationships expectations ought to be voiced out. If there is no clear communication of these needs and expectations, it is impossible for them to be met.

Expression of one's needs and expectations of each other and their relationship ought to be done in a friendly conversational manner; demanding one's expectations be met will only put his/her partner in a defensive state and lead to another argument between partners.

Irrespective of the level of connection between partners, they cannot completely agree on every issue. They are two different individuals, therefore it is expected that they will have different opinions and views on the same issue

In relationships, couples have a partnership in place that stipulates that they be emotionally and physically available for each other in times of need. However, the idea that one's partner will be readily available every time is a bit unrealistic. Individuals have their own sense of self outside their relationships, they have their own personal intrests, friends, extended family, career, etc. Although partners should try to be available for each other as often as possible, it is ludicrous for an individual to expect to be his/her partners sole focus.

• *Constant criticism*

In the same way an individual has e complaints xpectations from his/her relationship, there can also be and shortcomings. Humans are genetically flawed so a perfect behavior cannot and should not be expected from one's partner. However, the method used to relay shortcoming to one's partner is very important. When partners begin to accuse and assign blame to each other (who did what, who didn't do what, who said what, who didn't say what) the point they are trying to pass across becomes lost in translation as emotions begin to run high, feelings gets hurt, and partners begin a screaming match.

However, this could be avoided if partners share their complaints in a simple conversational manner without complaint and assigning blame.

• *Negative comparison, projection and stereotyping*

An individual's past relationships can affect and influence his/her behavior and attitudes towards new relationships and formation of emotional bonds. Conflicts can arise when partners allow past experiences to regulate their attitudes and perception of their current relationship. Comparing ones partner to other individuals reduces their self worth and gives them the illusion that their partners do not appreciate them. For example, a man who always compares his significant other to other more slender women will have his partner the idea that he does not find her attractive and wants to change her which may cause her to develop feelings of insecurity and resentment towards him.

In order to prevent conflicts and disagreements, Individuals with toxic past relationships have to take care not to project negative feelings from previous relationships into current relationship. This could lead to disagreement and conflict between current partners. New relationships should be entered into with a fresh start and partners with emotionally hurtful pasts should let go of negative feelings, give their new partner a chance to build intimacy and trust, without portraying feelings of insecurity and resentment from past relationships into the current one.

* *Ineffective communication and no sense of empathy*

When there is no free flow of communication and exchange of information between partners, it often leads to conflict and disagreements between them. Effective communications between partners helps them to understand each other better and prevent misinterpretations between them. When partners openly communicate, it inspires a sort of closeness between them, and then they understand each other's reasons for views and opinions and the reason behind certain actions. Likewise, when there is no open effective communication between partners, they jump to whatever conclusion they want to about each other, which gives them the wrong impression about their partners and gives room for misunderstanding and misinterpretation of intent.

When partners do not communicate about certain experiences and events and it's resulting feelings, there is no way for them to emphasize with each other. Without empathy in the relationship, partners are oblivious to each other's feelings and can hurt each other without meaning to. And in a relationship with no avenue for communication, there is no way for an individual to know his/her partner did not set out to cause hurt; the individual would think his/her partner is being hurtful on purpose and either put up emotional barriers between them or seek to hurt him/her back, thus continuing the vicious cycle.

WHAT ISSUES DO WE DISAGREE ON?

Understanding the specific issues causing disagreements in relationships can be a first step towards reconciliation of conflicts and disagreements. Partners in a committed relationship have an equal partnership and have to make every decision affecting their lived together. Because they are two entirely different individuals, the have different opinions and views about issues and if partners do not know how to effectively communicate his/her opinion and listen to and respect his/her partners opinion too even when they don't completely agree with them, there will be constant argument and conflict between them.

There are a million and one issues that can cause conflict and disagreements between partners and the solutions to these issues are equally that many. Partners can have disagreements on a number of issues ranging from what to have for dinner and to where to buy a house. Disagreements are a normal part of relationships; partners are encouraged to have different opinions about certain issues which helps them retain their self identity separate from the relationship, however this difference of opinion could lead to conflict between partners when both of them are unrelenting on said issue. The most effective way to resolve conflict between partners is through a system of compromise. Compromise involves a system of settlement of differences by consent reached through mutual concession. Compromise involves both partners agreeing on a midpoint between their differences where the decision reached equally serves both of them or serves none. Compromise entails settling differences in a win-win manner where both partner's needs are met. For example, a couple jointly buys a car, and can't agree on who gets to take the car to work since they work at opposite ends of the city. The obvious compromise choice in this case is that they get to take the car to work on a weekly shift basis. This way, both partners can be satisfied.

It is ideal to settle differences in a relationship using compromise because when partners compromise on issues and successfully arrive at a mid point that meets if not all but parts of an individual's needs, there is no aftermath feeling of resentment. During disagreements, the partner that always "loses " might begin to generate feelings of resentment towards his/her significant other. Regardless of the cause of argument or who is at fault and who is not, partners will always want to win the fight. There are no medals that one hopes to gain from winning fights or an argument with his/her partner but for the satisfaction and bragging rights of being right (I told you so). Not all arguments between partners are hostile. Some people like to argue to hear their partner's perspective on an issue and may not want to ask directly, thus he/she would incite an argument.

Partners bond on different levels. Some partners bond over shared interests, others bond over intellect, others bond as a result of physical attraction while some bond over the arguments they have. It is important to note that these types of arguments are without malice, and are more of argumentative conversations than disagreements.

There are also disagreements between partners that could be deal breakers for the both of them. In this cases, there are no compromises between partners; it's either all or nothing. In cases like this, both partners are unrelenting on their stands and the inability for partners to resolve these differences between could lead to termination of the relationship. The issues that themselves could lead to partners having an uncompromising arguments where both partners are unwilling to back down from their stands even at the risk of terminating their relationship are usually on life changing decisions. Some of such decisions may include deciding whether or not to fully commit and get married(In this cases, one partner feels the need to move the relationship to the next level and fully commit while the other partner is not quite there yet. The partner arguing for full commitment might give the other partner arguing against it an ultimatum to either get married or end the relationship.), whether or not to have children (in this case, one of the partners may not want to have children either due to financial reasons or underlying health issues or for fear of responsibility that children bring or because he/she is of the belief that having children would interfere with his/her career plan, while the other partner wants to focus on building a family and wants a child /children. To resolve this difference between them, one partner has to be willing to let go of his/her goal for the success of the relationship. Adoption cannot be seen as a point of compromise in this case because the individual that wants a child still wins even if he/she is not the birth parent.), whether or not to have a career(in this case, partners might have different opinions about gender specific roles, where the man thinks a woman's place is at home building the family, while the man provides and protects. The woman in the case might strongly object to that and want to build her own career and have her own source of income. In this case, the probability for compromise is considerably low and partners; if they do not find a common ground for compromise may terminate the relationship.

Some even argue that in cases like this, the reasonable thing to do is to terminate the relationship. This is because for partners to resolve the conflict and arrive at some sort of solution, one partner may have to give up on their core values which may lead to lose of self identity. For example, in the case of partners having different views on the roles of the man in the relationship and the roles of the woman in the relationship (gender specific roles), if the man gives up his socialized imprinted views of what a woman's role is in the family, he could be giving up core values that have been socialized into him from birth and if the woman gives up her career to stay back and build a home as her partner wants, she could lose her self identity as a strong self sufficient woman and become clinically depressed. Or in the case of different opinions on child bearing. If one partner gives up on the dream of building a family unit, he/she might later come to regret that decision and hold his/her partner accountable for the decision made. When if the other partner gives up an agrees to have a child he/she does not want, their attitude towards the child might be one of indifference and neglect which will affect the child emotionally and mentally. Also, in cases where one partner is pressured into a committed relationship (marriage) when he/she is not emotionally, mentally and physically ready for it, such an individual may begin to resent his/her partner and go through the relationship half-assed, which may cause them to drift apart emotionally and eventually terminate the relationship.

Therefore, in cases like this where compromise cannot be reached, partners may want to reconsider the relationship rather than lose their values or self identity.

HOW DO WE RECONNECT AND MAINTAIN INTIMACY AFTER RESOLVING CONFLICT?

Maintain intimacy is crucial for the success of every long term relationship. Existing intimacy between partners helps both partners to understand each other, identify unspoken feelings of hurt faster and to better empathize with each other. It is relatively easier to identify partners with a strong sense of intimacy between them, There is usually a sync of communication between them, understanding without explanation, constant show of affection like touching as often as possible, holding hands, and a sense of togetherness between them.

Creating and maintaining emotional intimacy requires genuine interest, transparency, vulnerability and reciprocity. The degree of intimacy in a relationship is determined by the ability to listen to and understand one's partner. Couples in an intimate relationship must develop genuine interest to create intimacy and be willing to lower their emotional barriers and be vulnerable with each other. It is important for partners to be intimate with each other and to have intimate knowledge of one another to smoothly coexist together. This is not to say that partners with emotional intimacy between them do not experience the occasional emotional disconnection, disagreement on issues and conflict.

Both emotional bond and connection and physical bond and connections suffer when there is a conflict between partners. This is because emotional intimacy creates an emotional bond between partners which helps them to understand each other better on a deeper level. However, when there is a break emotional bonds, as a result of conflicts and disagreements, partners tend to drift apart from each other and their relationship and their emotional connection stretches and eventually breaks. There is an elasticity on the emotional connections between partners which is determined by the level of emotional intimacy between them. The deeper the level of emotional intimacy between partners, the stronger elasticity of their emotional connection. The emotional connection elasticity is the degree to which intimate partners relationship could withstand wear and tear. The band of elasticity of partners emotional connection, eventually contracts and bring drifting partners back together in harmony and intimacy. Minor disagreements and conflict of interest between partners can easily be withstood by the emotional connection elasticity, however, when partners engage in a major conflict and disagreements where there were hardly any room for compromise, partners might drift father and father away from each other for the emotional connection elasticity to pull them back together. When this happens, the emotional connection between partners break and emotional intimacy is lost. After conflict is resolved between partners and partners seek to rebuild the emotional intimacy lost between them, there is a need to reestablish lost emotional connection between partners in an attempt to open up one's mind and stir up feelings necessary for rebuilding emotional intimacy.

There need to be an open line of effective communication for reconnecting partners looking to rebuild emotional intimacy. Although partners already have working knowledge of each other due to their previously existing intimacy, they need to build another link; a fresh start between them without blemish of past disagreement and conflict. This does not mean partners should forget about previous disagreements and conflict; in contrary, they should remember it and use it as a guideline to avoiding similar occurrences in the near future. In a bid to rebuild intimacy and reconnect their relationship, partners need to openly converse with each other, share their complaints and truest feelings about issues affecting their relationship especially about how certain issues in the previous disagreements made them feel. The aim of this is to reopen the line of effective communication between partners, giving them an opportunity to fully express how certain experiences in the previous disagreements made them feel, to encourage empathy and rebuild trust between them. In the course of this open conversations, partners should bring up the events and experiences that led up to the previous disagreement and conflict, not to assign blames but in a effort to work through any negative residual feelings towards each other and work towards rebuilding their relationship. This problem solving conversation should be held in a conversational not accusatory manner to help partners see from each other's perspective. Burying down negative residual feelings from the disagreement and conflict will only provide a temporary fix from the problem and would arise again and again at a later date to cause more problems unless they are resolved immediately. Therefore, partners need to have intimate conversations about resulting feelings from previous conflict in order to settle differences.

During conflict, a lot of degrading languages may have been used in the heat of the moment, which may have deeply offended one or both partners. There is a need to partners to own up to their mistakes and offer an apology to each other and to other parties involved in the disagreement.

The road to building intimacy is a slow steady one, it is even slower when attempting to rebuild intimacy because partners may not be as willing to develop trust for each other again after disagreement. If both partners are determined to rebuild intimacy and reconnect their

entanglement relationship, they would have to exercise patience and aim at building emotional intimacy first before attempting to redefine their relationship on a fresh slate.

Lastly, in a bid to rebuild intimacy and reconnect strangled relationship, partners should put a proposal forward to reconnect the relationship, then give each other some space to decide whether they both want to reconnect the relationship or not. entanglement did not happen overnight, reconnecting the relationship too would not happen overnight; partners need to give each other space to make the right decision without influencing whatever decision his/her partner makes with their presence. Reconnecting the relationship is basically giving the relationship a second chance; individuals need to be sure if they are emotional capable to try again with his/her partner, albeit in a new redefined relationship/ partnership.

WHEN CONVERSATIONS GROW STALE, HERE ARE SOME FUN QUESTIONS FOR PARTNERS TO ASK EACH OTHER.

As earlier stated, mutually answered questions and intimate conversations are the major tools in building and maintaining emotional intimacy between partners and reconnecting relationships. However, when partners have successfully attained a deep level of emotional intimacy with his/her partner through asking all the necessary questions required to building emotional intimacy, and conversation between them becomes stale, below are some intriguing questions partners could mutually answer to open up new areas of conversation.

What is your idea of a perfect relationship / or day?

What would you change if you had the power to change one thing about yourself permanently? And why?

What is your favorite childhood memory?

What was your unrealistic childhood dream?

How different would your life have been from present state if those dreams had come true?

What is your biggest fear? And why?

What is the one thing you want to do before you die?

Where is the one place you want to visit before you die?

What was your first life defining moment?

If you had the power to switch bodies with anyone in the world for a fee days, who would you want to be for a few days?

when did you first experience pure joy and why?

What would you do or not do if you could go back 15 years?

What scent makes you think of me?

What is your spirit animal? And why?

What is your idea of fun?

When was the last time you were wildly spontaneous?

What do you think my spirit animal is?

What was your first impression of me? What changed your mind?

What are you " shameful " vices?

If you could get three wishes granted, what would they be?

These questions are purely hypothetical and have no bearing whatsoever on reality. They however, could lead up to meaningful conversations between partners which could help them in creating, maintaining emotional intimacy abd reconnect relationships.

CONCLUSION

"our soul craves intimacy " - Erwin Raphael Mcmanus.

Individuals have a genetic need for intimacy and closeness and they seek to build intimacy with people closest to them like one's immediate family, childhood best friend, Romantic partners, etc.

Individuals seeking to build intimacy with their partners need to understand the type of emotional connection building intimacy between partners requires. For intimacy to be built between partners, both partners have to be willing participants and work towards building intimacy together. This process strengthens the emotional bond between both partners, because the journey to building and maintaining emotional intimacy can also be seen as a shared goal between them. The functions of emotional intimacy in relationships cannot be over emphasized; emotional intimacy gives an individual the feeling of belonging to something special, something bigger than himself/ herself, an entity old as time itself; Love.

When we love someone and are accepted by them, it is natural to want to be as close to them as possible, therefore we seek to form intimacy with them. Through intimacy, we mix certain private aspects of our lives with that of the person we are seeking to form intimacy with.

Creating intimacy does not just happen over night. When we create emotional bonds with people, it does not necessarily mean we had created intimacy with them; creating intimacy goes a little further than that. When partners are intimate with each other, there is an utter sense of vulnerability, openness and trust between that that allows them to share normally hidden aspects of themselves with each other, without fear of judgment or condemnation. As a result of the deep level of trust needed to create and maintain intimacy, individuals need to be highly selective in choosing partners to be intimate with. In order to prevent an individual from creating intimacy with an emotionally unstable person which will go on to hurt him/her, an individual has to reach a deeper understanding of who his/her partner is, what motivates them, their history and background, their perception of relationships and everything pertaining to making a successful long lasting relationship, their relationship expectations, their influences, their behavioral and personality traits, their values, hope, dreams and goals, their defining moment and experiences, their past partners and relationships, their conflict resolution techniques and attitude, their self identity and awareness , etc.

In summary, for an individual to build intimacy with his/her partner, such an individual need to know who his/her partner and attain a deeper level of understanding about their perception of self and life in general. The aim of this book is to guide individuals on questions partners looking to build emotional intimacy to ask each other that will initiate open effective communication that would help them know each other better and build intimacy between them if they wish it.

Partners that have drifted apart emotionally from each other too could use this set of questions to understand the cause of the emotional distance between them and mutually answering these questions, could lead to open conversations that would help them reconnect in their relationship and build emotional intimacy between them.

NOTE

Building emotional intimacy is a delicate step by step process. It requires patience, careful consideration, keen observation, and a good judgment for an individual to select an ideal candidate from numerous prospects to build emotional intimacy with. The presence of emotional intimacy between partners deepens the relationship and connection between them, thus making them more vulnerable, and open to hurt and

helpless betrayal. Because of this underlying risks and need for trust, individuals have to be careful and extremely picky in selecting suitable partners to form an emotional intimate bond with. This involves picking emotionally stable and reliable partners in whom trust can be fully placed without fear. Although there are no guarantees in relationships, Selecting an emotional stable partner greatly reduces the risks of emotional turmoil in the future.

The process of selection is effectively done through asking questions and initiating revealing conversations. Asking questions could serve a double purpose of getting to know if one's selected partner is suitable to form an emotionally intimate relationship with, and also starts the process of building emotional intimacy between partners by helping them to get to know each other better through mutually answered questions.

In reconnecting relationships, asking and mutually answering questions help partners to reach a deeper level of understanding with each other by revealing little hidden knowledge about each other that they had probably missed or forgotten about each other.

Asking these questions and initiating these conversations help partners truly see and understand each other, which strengthens their emotional bond and connection.

It is important to note that partners seeking to build emotional intimacy and reconnect their relationship, both have to be willing to ask and answer these questions. It is a give and take process.

© Written by: Katerina Griffith

www.ingramcontent.com/pod-product-compliance
Lightning Source LLC
Chambersburg PA
CBHW070122290526
45789CB00005B/2112